REFUGEE

FROM AFGHANISTAN

No one wants to leave her home… or loved ones… UNLESS SHE MUST

ASMEEN HAMKAR

*When refugees arrive on your soil, help them
to restart their life again. Do not close your
door on them. They seek refugee in you.*

Listen to them.

Each one has a story to tell.

TABLE OF CONTENTS

CHAPTER ONE

The darkness of the night slowly made its journey toward daylight.

That was the longest night of my life. Minutes crawled....

I paced from one side of the room to the other, back and forth, monitoring the clock that hung on the wall to make sure it was working, wishing for daylight. Finally, the clock struck 4 AM; but it was still dark.

My heart started beating faster; my entire body was bathed in fear. Agha-jan (my name for my father) and I impatiently waited for the darkness of the long night to turn to daylight so we could leave our home. I could wait no longer. Impatiently, I wished for wings to fly to the sky like a bird from a cage. I paced and paced in the small room, counting the minutes.

Out the window, I could see the sky slightly changing from dark to light gray.

Agha-jan and I opened our apartment door, stepped down the stairs and walked through the foyer to the main entrance which was left wide open. It seemed someone left before us and did not shut the main door, or someone came in to hide from the neighborhood.

We stepped out of the building, and immediately a cold breeze touched my face. That was one of the coldest winter nights on record in Kabul, the capital of Afghanistan[1]. Trees around our apartment building were decorated with crystal beads, each one adorned like a bride with a white dress.

Even though our neighborhood looked so beautiful and welcoming, the atmosphere was full of fear and horror.

There were no birds chirping; it was deadly quiet. The neighborhood looked strange. Changes had been encompassing our neighborhood for the past few years as the government regime kept constantly changing from fair to bad, from bad to worse, and from worse to extreme. Even Mother Nature was afraid to raise her voice. If Mother Nature was afraid to speak out, then what could her lowly inhabitant do? I took a deep breath and asked myself, "How can we leave our beautiful home, our neighborhood, our hometown, our country?" Those were the questions that I still cannot find answers for.

Agha-jan and I were the last people from my family to leave our home which was crumbling around us. Our poor home did not look like a home anymore: no windows, no doors, and no roof. It was demolished.

---

[1] **Afghanistan** is a landlocked country in Asia. It is bordered by Pakistan to the east and south; Iran to the west; Turkmenistan, Uzbekistan, and Tajikistan to the north; and China to the northeast. Occupying 652,000 square kilometers (252,000 sq mi), it is a mountainous country with plains in the north and southwest. Kabul is the capital and largest city. The population is 32 million, mostly composed of ethnic Pashtuns, Tajiks, Hazaras and Uzbeks.

My home knew that it could not shelter us anymore; it could not keep us safe there anymore. It knew that we lost our belongings and our loved ones there. My beautiful home looked so quiet, but I felt like I was abandoning a friend. I felt it voicelessly asking me, "Why are you leaving me?" I felt it asked itself, "Why did they hurt me? Why did they beat me up?" The rebels destroyed my home brick by brick. Burning doors, smashing windows, leveling walls to make a point that my home, my sanctuary was meaningless. "What did I do to them? Not me nor my owner belonged to any social or political groups. We were enemy to no one. Why did they do this to my neighborhood?"

My beautiful home did not want to see us suffering any more. It did not want to be a witness to anymore suffering, pain and horror. It could not talk, but in its silence, it beckoned us: "Get a move on before they stop you. Go, before they kill you. Go, I am not safe for you anymore; I cannot hide you behind my injured walls. Please go; safety is waiting for you somewhere. Go fast, before they get you, before they kill you."

I was singing in my head, "How can I leave you? How can I leave you?" while I walked behind my Agha-jan.[2] Agha-jan was always strong, even though he had been injured like our home. He was wounded by a large piece of shrapnel lodged in his back from an attack on our home during the war in Afghanistan.

That day he was suffering from pain, but he was trying to survive. My Agha-jan's heart was so broken. It had

---

[2] In Afghanistan, it is the culture that women do not walk in front of their father, brother, husband or, in some cases, son. It is a way of respecting and acknowledging the men's authority in the society.

not been that long ago that he lost his loved ones, his
beautiful wife, beautiful daughter, and beautiful son.
His home was destroyed. He lost his job and lost every
aspect of his deep beliefs. He was the only one that I
could rely on, my supporter and my bearer, even though
he was sick, injured and was carrying that huge load
of sorrow and pain. With all that pain, he was trying to
survive to be there for me. Agha-jan was my hero, my
life, and he meant everything to me.

We left our apartment, but we did not know where
we would end up. The only thing that we knew at
that time was that we needed to leave Kabul. But the
whole of Afghanistan was suffering from the horror of
war. No matter if we lived in Kabul or another city, it
would be the same. Afghan people, especially women,
faced systematic human rights abuses, demotion, and
discrimination. Women were required to cover from
head to toe when in public. They were not allowed
to work any type of job or have access to any type of
education system.

As soon as Agha-jan and I left our apartment building
and found our way to the main street, we saw a group
of people ahead of us, walking in the same direction as
us.

We immediately knew our goal was the same: we were
on the same journey. People were leaving their homes
daily in seek of safety. That day it was our turn. We
made that decision not knowing what was ahead of us
or what could happen; but with Gods' support, we were
praying we would find a safe place.

The crowd of people were walking as fast as they
could. Women wore big scarfs, covered from head to

toe with 'chadari,' also known as a 'burka.'[3] Men wore hats or turbans with long beards, and kids wore multiple layers of clothing trying to keep warm. Nothing in their hands. People could not carry anything with them, because they didn't want to be identified as individuals evacuating their homes or the country. Instead of travel baggage, everyone was carrying big loads of fear and expecting the worst at any time. They were walking quickly in order to leave the city where the Taliban Militias were patrolling from time to time.

Agha-jan and I tried to get closer to the crowd of people on the icy road. My mind was still at home, before war destroyed it and took our happiness. My mind was with my beautiful clothes, my school supplies, my books, my bed, the leaves of the Sinjid tree[4] outside of our apartment that reached to my bedroom window, and many more memories of things that I left behind and that were very hard to forget.

Every minute, I thought my home was calling me to come back: "I will be there for you like before." I thought my mother was watching us with her beautiful smile and waving good bye; I thought my brother was

---

[3] Traditional clothing in Afghanistan is generally loose-fitting and conservative. Women historically wear clothes that covered them: a dress with loose-fitting pants (tunbaan) reaching the ankles. A headscarf called *chador* is worn to cover the hair. Outside of their homes, they used *chadari* to cover from head to toe. In the1960s, women at work or at college wore modern clothing. But a generation before them, their mothers or grandmothers dressed traditionally. Every Afghan was fully aware of traditional clothes for men and women. But, as the world moved toward modernization, Afghan women also wanted to follow the world. They started dressing modernly in 1960, and the government never forced them to cover. Throughout Afghan history, women's rights have varied; but officially, Afghan women gained equality under the 1964 constitution. Then in the civil war in the 1990s, Taliban took away the Afghan women's rights and forced them to cover from head to toe.

[4] Elaeagnus angustifolia is commonly known as Persian olive or wild olive. It's commonly referred to as Senjid or Sinjid in Afghanistan and Senjed in Iran. It is a species native to Afghanistan, from southern Russia and Kazakhstan to Turkey and Iran.

looking at me and wanted to tell me not to go; I thought my beautiful sister with her beautiful green eyes was watching me and wanted to hug me good bye. Those thoughts kept repeating in my imagination; and in my ears, I heard repeating, "When will you be back? When will you return?"

We got closer and blended into the crowd. Among the people on the road, I saw a couple of our distant relatives who were in the same boat as us. Seeing them, I felt stronger and more energized, and I thought to myself, "We are not alone leaving my hometown; other people have the same goal as us." We walked and walked, passing one road after another, one village after another, until we reached Bagrami, a town on the eastern fringes of Kabul.

We arrived at the Bagrami Valley mid-morning. It was my first trip to Bagrami, but it was not so different from other little towns or villages in the area. Houses with tall walls around them, wide paved roads, little shops here and there. The crowd stopped to get some water from a young boy who was handing out water from a big teapot outside his house.

Hospitably is one big part of Afghan culture, no matter from which tribe and what region you come. The young boy treated us as his guests since we were passing their valley. He probably saw these kinds of crowds passing their valley so often. Aside from culture, from the Islamic religious perspective, if you give drinking water to thirsty people, God will grant you forgiveness.

While people rushed to get drinking water, Agha-jan showed me that his shoes were falling apart. The soles of his shoes were separating from the rest of the shoe.

I looked at his shoes and did not know what to do. I felt helpless and lost. His shoes were not winter shoes, so they could not tolerate a long walk, in winter. We couldn't find anything to wrap around his shoes to keep them together for now. He had no other choice; he had no other shoes.

The crowd started walking again. Agha-jan walked in those tattered shoes through the mud, dust and rubble. Taking one step at a time, mile after mile.

We arrived at another village and saw a few men from neighboring streets standing outside their gates watching this caravan of people coming from Kabul seeking safety.

Agha-jan asked one of the men standing around if they had an extra pair of shoes they would be willing to give him. One of them asked him to wait while he went into the house and returned with a pair of shoes that looked very foreign to me. I think they were either a size 11 or 12. The shoes were made of wood! They were a sight! I had never seen wooden shoes before.

Agha-jan had difficulty walking in them. He said they were from a very long time ago, maybe even a hundred years ago. Those shoes looked like they were made in the first century.

My father took the shoes and wore them throughout our journey. His feet were dirty from the mud and dust. I do not think they were very comfortable, but I do not recall him complaining. He just kept going.

Agha-jan was very strong and resilient. He went through a very difficult life: lost his two beautiful children, lost his lovely wife, lost his warm home, and was injured. So walking with old broken-down wooden shoes on a muddy crumbled road was nothing compared to what he had been through in his life.

Once we passed through Bagrami, we reached the Pole-Charkhi road connecting to the highway that would lead us out of Kabul City, allowing us to escape the danger while the entire country was heading toward annihilation.

Pole-Charkhi is the Afghan National Detention facility. It is the largest prison in Kabul. This facility was constructed during president Daoud Khan's government in 1970s. I did not want to look at its gray buildings with narrow windows, because it reminded me of the time when my brother was there during the communist regime. I had a lot of fear, heartache, and hopelessness; and entering that road added to my load of pain and reminded me of difficult days from the past.

We continued walking on Pole-Charkhi road. It was a long walk from early morning to almost afternoon over paved, rubbled, muddy, and icy roads. We were walking together in fear and horror. No hope, no safety. We did not know what would happen to us from minute to minute.

We were very hungry and thirsty. We walked until I had no feeling in my legs. They felt like two stumps trudging along going nowhere. My entire body was so drained, but stretching out in front of us was the main road. I urged every bone in my body to keep going faster, faster: there was hope.

When we got closer, we saw a tractor with a trailer, and people rushed to jump on. Agha-jan and I willed our bodies forward and got into the back of the trailer. The trailer was full of people, men, women, and children. I sat on the floor with the others, while my father stood by the gate.

We were packed in like bricks in a wall. The trailer rolled along over the muddy, icy Pole-Charkhi road toward the main highway, where we hoped to find a ride to bring us to the southern provinces of Afghanistan.

The snow started coming down. It was bitter cold outside. The snow fell on my face, touching my eyes and my cheeks. It was so beautiful, clean, and white. The tractor rumbled along loudly. People in the open trailer were almost completely covered by the fresh snowfall on their heads and shoulders. We were getting closer and closer to the highway; we did not know what would happen next.

The major highway we saw in the distance links Kabul to Nangarhar (Jalalabad) province, running next to the Kabul and Kunar rivers. When we got closer to the highway, we saw a few minibuses parked next to the road to pick up passengers traveling to Jalalabad. The bumpy cold highway traveled through the mountains, and our hope was that the minibuses would take us to Jalalabad, the border city, where we could cross the border and leave Afghanistan.

People jumped out of the trailer in a rush to get into the minibuses. We hurried over to a minibus, looking for the driver to open the doors and let us in. It was snowing, cold, and in the middle of nowhere.
I cannot remember how I got in the minibus. The only

thing I recall was the force of the crowd pushing me towards the bus doors while they were trying to find a seat for themselves. In the blink of an eye, I found myself in the bus. But I couldn't see my Agha-jan! I started yelling, "Agha-jan, Agha-jan, where are you?" I kept calling for my Agha-jan.

And then I heard a faint tired voice from behind me saying, "Don't worry, don't worry. I am here." I thanked God and told myself I would never allow myself to be separated from him again.

The minibuses were filled by the escaping crowd looking for freedom and safety. We all were tired, hungry, and freezing. The driver yelled, "In the name of God, have a safe trip." We were off.

The situation was not new to the minibus drivers. They experienced this deluge of people daily, transporting people from an outpost in the middle of nowhere to Jalalabad city. The bus was crowed. People sat or stood in every open space they could find. Children were crying, asking for food. Everyone was physically and emotionally drained.

In a short while, we passed through the Surobi district and its tunnel. We passed through the dark tunnel with the Kabul River looming at the bottom of the rocky mountains.

The Kabul River starts its journey from the bottom of the Paghman Mountains toward the south. It flows in an easterly direction, past Kabul through Jalalabad city. It then moves on to Dakka, where it enters Pakistani territory, finally running into the Indus River at Attock . The convergence of the Kabul river and the Indus river create an interesting and beautiful view. Half of the river water looks blue, and the other half looks gray. It runs like this until it disappears from sight.

I was watching the beautiful landscape of Afghanistan, from the rocky mountains to the raging rivers breaking waves on the big stones, moving faster than us as we rumbled along the crumbling highway to escape danger and to escape my beautiful home, Afghanistan.

With every passing moment, we were distancing ourselves from Kabul City, where I was born. For the first time in my life, a whole new world was before me. Kabul, one of thirty-four provinces, is situated in the eastern part of Afghanistan. The capital of the province is Kabul, which is also the capital of Afghanistan. At the time we left, Kabul City was suffering from an imposed pain. The city was mourning the loss of hundreds and hundreds of its people. Young, old, men, women, and children. The city had lost the cultural and historical values of its past.

All the historical spires, such as Maiwond Victory Monument (built in 1959 to commemorate the Battle of Maiwond in 1880 when the Afghans were victorious over the British in the Second Anglo Afghan War) and many more, were either destroyed or closed. Many other historical and cultural treasures, such as the Kabul museum, Darul-Aman Palace, and Tajbik Palace, were looted or destroyed. The historical city of Kabul was hardly touched. The Taliban were more interested in erasing culture and heritage. The smoke billowed continuously in the sky as, one by one, major cultural buildings were destroyed.

The ruined city was depressing, witnessing the pain, sorrow, suffering and escape of its people who did not know where they were going - north, south, east, or west. There were very few options for the Kabuli residents: try to find a way to the south east side of town in order to escape into Pakistan, or try to find a way to the north side of town to escape into Uzbekistan or Tajikistan.

During the Mujahidin war from 1992 to 1996, Kabul City witnessed masses of people flooding into the city, bloody, dying with no help in sight. Hospitals were overcrowded and doctors and nurses in short supply. During the Taliban from 1996 to 2001, there were no hospitals and medical providers. There would be no help, and people died.

We left our home with the hope of arriving at a safe place, a place to breathe normally, a place to lay our heads and sleep with no fear; a place to see the sunshine; a place to live a normal life again without horror and fear.

Our minibus was running on the Kabul Jalalabad Highway. I looked at the Kabul River from the bus window, dreaming of our happy family, beautiful home, school days, and loving friends. As we went further and further from the ruined city, I realized that everything was gone. All I saw was a silent river.

The sun was slowly dropping down behind the mountain, as if it were trying to hide. It was replacing the long day with an even longer night. We were about to experience our first night away from home under strangers' rooves or maybe somewhere under the beautiful sky. Our bus arrived at Jalalabad City, a large city in the Eastern part of Afghanistan. A beautiful city mostly famous for its orange and palm trees, Jalalabad did not experience the war as bad as Kabul; but still it was not safe, because it was under the dominance of the Taliban regime. It frightened me that I could still hear the voices of fear and horror even here, so far east.

We spent the night in Jalalabad at the house of my cousin Fahima's in-law, we happened to have met on the way from Kabul. In earlier days, he and his family had spent winters in Jalalabad in this house (since Jalalabad has a warm climate in winter) and spent summers in Kabul. But now he had moved his family to Pakistan for safety and had come back to sell some of his properties in Kabul for money to support his family in Pakistan. But with all the uncertainty in Kabul and the entire Country, no one was willing to buy anything. The only priority for people was their safety, not business or investment. He luckily was able to rent out his home here to local tenants. The tenants were welcoming, nice, country people who eagerly rushed to serve us food cooked on an open fire that filled the air with smoke. I was so hungry; I devoured my plate of meat and rice and drank my tea, warming my body and soul.

As is the Afghan country people's tradition, the women ate in one room and the men ate in another when they had guests. I didn't want to be separated from my Agha-jan, but tradition is tradition. I happily chatted with the other women in Pashto and in Dari. As we talked, I felt relaxed and silently laid my head down on some pillows next to me. They warmly told me to be comfortable and rest well. As my tired eyes slowly closed, I noticed the old oil lamp burning in the corner of the room. Its glass was half dark from the smoke which made half of the room dark, and other half softly lit. The flickering of the lamp seemed to say to me, "Shut your tired eyes and go to sleep. Sleep well; you are still here, in Afghanistan." I was so tired. I dreamt of shadows and ghosts that haunt me to this day.

Tomorrow would continue our difficult journey, which meant crossing an international border. Who knew what would happen to us. Could we cross the border? Could we escape? What if the Taliban caught us? What if they tortured Agha-jan in front of my eyes? What if they tortured me in front of him? What if they killed us? If we could cross the border, we would be leaving my country, and I prayed that all would be well.

The next day I woke up early and went to the balcony. The sky looked different to me, very blue, very clear; the sunshine was so relaxing. They had a beautiful yard, country style, so many trees. Their kitchen was outside of the building. They used a wood oven to cook and boil the water to make tea. I saw the host wife came out of the cow's barn. She had a bucket of very fresh cow's milk with her; she had just milked the cow. She was so brave! She had milked the cow herself! I softly said to myself, "Oh my God, I even cannot pass by the cow." I felt bad that she was working so hard, so I decide to go and help her make the breakfast. I found my way to the yard and to the kitchen. She said, with a beautiful smile, "Do not come to the kitchen, because the wood oven is lit and makes lots of smoke. You are a city girl; you cannot tolerate the smoke."

I said, "No, I really want to help you. I saw you milked the cow!"

She said with a very smiley face, "Yes, it is my routine every day." Then I saw her recover the dough pot, and she said, "It is ready to make bread."

After seeing that she had another big project, I said, "For sure I cannot help her, because I never baked bread in a wood oven." I left their kitchen. The smoke made my eyes burn and water. As I was on my way back to the building, I looked at my shoes that were so muddy from the walking yesterday. I got a stick, sat on their stairs, and separated the dry mud from my shoes to make them ready for rest of our journey.

That morning we had a very delicious breakfast like I have never had since. Fresh milk, hot homemade bread, clear red tea, with fried eggs from their chicken. Everything was so fresh and so tasty. But we must leave. We thanked them a lot for letting us stay with them in their house.

We continued our trip, heading toward Pakistan. We had to take another bus to the border, but before that Agha-jan needed to buy shoes. On the side of street, we saw a cart full of plastic shoes for men, women, and kids. Agha-jan went toward that cart and bought a pair of plastic shoes for himself. Those shoes were not to his standard; but at that time he could not afford to buy something that normally he wore, so he had to buy those shoes.

Crossing into Pakistan was scary. We arrived at the border after a couple hours' bus ride. We started walking toward mountains. As we walked, fear walked side by side with us. We did not know whether we could cross the border or not.

We spent that morning crossing the high mountains of Khyber Pass. The natural beauty immediately caught my eye. The green rocky mountains felt fresh and clean. I was looking at them with interest but with ambiguity. These mountains were not my beloved country.

We arrived at Khyber Pakhtunkhwa, a border town between Afghanistan and Pakistan. As soon as we crossed the border, I started to feel strange. Strange to the beckoning nature, strange to the fresh air, and strange to myself. It was not me; it was someone else. A person with an empty heart, a person who did not know where life was taking her, a person who had lost herself among those mountains.

We crossed the border into Pakistan. We arrived in Peshawar city. Peshawar was crowded with people busily going about their normal life. It was the second day of my journey and my first day in Pakistan.

In fact, my journey begins from that day.

CHAPTER TWO

My feet were burning with pain, as if I was walking
on sharp glass or cactus. The city buses were full of
people. The shops and supermarkets were open. Music
filled the air and lights were coming on. One could
forget that we had fled our home, with all this wonder
around us.

We passed by restaurants with the wonderful smell
of spices and cooking kabab. Languages filling the
air - Pashto and Urdu. Their Pashto accent sounded
so different to me. A vibrant culture and environment
swirled around in front of me.

I felt that everyone was staring at us. We were strangers
to them, unwanted, uninvited. We had a different
culture, language and clothing, and we looked ragged.
We were refugees from a war-torn country.

Some called us Afghans (Afghani or Khan), but for
the most part they called us 'Muhajreen,' which means
refugees, people in search of safety. Pakistan became
a host country for Afghan refugees in the 1970s during
the Soviet invasion. Its people got used to seeing
undocumented Afghans in their cities and country.

But hosting did not mean that Afghans had the same rights as the Pakistani people. Afghans did not have the right to work or purchase houses or cars or have a bank account. Afghan kids born in Pakistan were not allowed to attend public schools or universities. They lived there waiting to be deported to Afghanistan, a country where they had never been.

That evening we went to our relatives' home who had been living in Peshawar since the communist regime ruled Afghanistan. We showed up at their door without any prior notice. As soon as they saw us, they expressed their happiness that we were alive and were able to leave Afghanistan.

We stayed with them for a few weeks. They were gracious, but we knew it was an inconvenience for them. They had two small rooms with a small kitchen, bathroom, and courtyard. The addition of two more tired bodies to their current family of fourteen was not so welcome. The house was already too small for them; but they were most gracious and let Agha-jan and me sleep in their home.

For me, it was so difficult to sleep in the same room as a few grown up boys. At night, the floor of each room was covered with Afghan mattress made of cotton. Everyone found a mattress to sleep on. My hope every night was to get a mattress next to the wall; at least from one side, I would not hear snoring.

The first couple of nights, as soon as it got dark, I went to sleep. But the third night, this was not the case. I was awake almost all night. My feet were still very sore. My mind was very lost; I did not know what to think about.

We were alive; we were safe; but we had nothing to live on.

Nothing belonged to us; we did not belong to anything.

The air, the land, the water, the country, the city, the house, the room, the mattress, and pillow - nothing was mine.

The new chapter of my life started from that moment. I told myself, "Put all the fear behind you and move forward."

The next morning, I tried to read our hosts' minds about our stay in their home. Of course, what I read was right: they wanted to know how long we would be staying with them. But we did not know.

Agha-jan and I did not want to stay there longer, but we had no other option; where could we go? They knew what we were going through. They had been refugees themselves and knew the hardships we were facing. Even though they had been living in Pakistan for over 10 years, they still felt like outsiders. More than one decade of their life was spent in complete uncertainty, and only God knew how much longer that uncertainty would continue.

At that time there were a few refugee camps in Pakistan. The nearest camp was called Nasir Bagh. It was in horrible condition, unsafe and infested with snakes, scorpions, and more. Most of those camps were occupied by Afghan refugees that left Afghanistan during the communist regime. Many of those people came from the southern provinces of Afghanistan, mainly country people with low education. Nasir Bagh was in the desert; a dirty canal passed through the area. People used the water for drinking and cooking. There was no electricity or medical attention.

Since most refugees in Nasir Bagh were refugees that lived there for decades, they felt that camp belonged to them, that they owned the area. They made that place very unsafe for newcomers to live. So, we couldn't even think about living in there. On the other hand, we felt uncomfortable stretching our relatives' kindness and staying with them for so long.

This was a rough time for Agha-jan and me. This was the first time in our life that we experienced dependence on others. Sometimes we felt we would rather live in the refugee camp than with our relatives.

One day, by chance, Agha-jan ran into a school friend of my brother, Obaidullah, in a very busy market. He was selling cigarettes and matches to make money to support his family. He was Obaidullah's good friend. He had come to our house on exam nights, when he and Obaidullah studied together.

Back then, when I was a little girl, I loved to help my mother, and my sister, Samia, with the house work, but there was none for me to do, really. So, I found the broom and would sweep the sidewalks in our yard. That made me so proud of myself, that I did something around the house. I would boss around and tell people to not make the sidewalk dirty because I cleaned it. My brother's friend, Abdul, knew that; whenever he came to our house with his bicycle, right at the entrance door, he made sure to let me know that he was not making the sidewalk dirty. He called to me,

"Little Sister, look, my shoes and my bicycle tires are clean. I washed them before I came here!"

He and his family were able to escape from Afghanistan a few months before us. He asked Agha-jan where we lived and when we had arrived. As soon as he heard about our living conditions, Abdul said, "Come and live with me and my family until you find a job and get your own place to live." Agha-jan agreed. He preferred to live with Abdul and his family and leave our relatives' house.

The next day we moved to his little home. Abdul and his family lived in one room of an unfinished old house in an area called Board. The crumbling walls were very scary, and I wondered if they would hold up.

The roof was made of plastic, making the house look even more precarious. I always felt that the roof would collapse at any time. Even though the situation of the family was clearly difficult, they were very welcoming and were always so gracious. Sleeping arrangements were very clear. The women and children would sleep inside of the room, while the men slept in the courtyard. The first night in their home, I felt very comfortable sleeping the in room with women and children. No relatives' grown-up boys!

The area was not as safe as my relatives' house, so, each night someone kept watch on the family while the others slept. Living with this family was much better for us. Even though our addition made the husband sleep outside, they were still so nice to me and my father. They were supportive of us and cared for us so much.

Not long after we moved in with them, they received a notice from their landlord that they must vacate that little house. The new owners were planning to finish constructing that house.

We were potentially homeless again! Abdul and his family were so sad that they were about to lose their free living space. We decided to start looking for a place to live, a cheap place that we could afford. We thought we could find a place to live together and share expenses. At the time, we did not have any jobs and no income. The only thing we had was hope to find a job and regain our self-confidence.

The next morning, Abdul's wife and I started looking for a place to rent. Our goal was to find an affordable place with at least two bedrooms. On the second day of our search, we found a two-bedroom house! We were all thrilled! The house was very old and in questionable condition. It had been vacant for a long time. Not good, but ok enough for now. The train track passed just in front of this house, and whenever the train was passing, the entire house shook! That was not important for us at that time. The only thing important was that it was better than living in the camp or in the relatives' house. Agha-jan and Abdul agreed to get that house and share the rent, 200.00 rupees a month.

Soon we moved into the little house. Agha-jan and I had our own space, our own room with a roof made of tree branches and leaves. There was a big old wooden window frame, but no window glass, and a very old wooden door with lots of open cracks. The walls were half painted; the rest of the paint was gone due to humidity. The floor was right on the ground. That small room was such a meaningful step for us.

Right at this time, my oldest uncle, who lived in the U.S., sent us two hundred dollars. Wow! Two hundred dollars! That day we went to bazar and bought clothes, hygiene items, cooking utensils, food, and a sewing machine.

In the old days in Afghanistan, Agha-jan owned a tailoring shop as a side job. In fact, he designed and sewed all the clothing of a famous and historic movie actress, Rabia Balkhi. Now he bought that sewing machine to work and make money to support us. He still suffered from pain. And we, like a million other Afghan that lived in Pakistan, had no documentation and no work authority.

Soon after we settled in our home, Agha-jan posted a sign on the courtyard door, "Women's Tailoring." We were hopeful neighboring people would bring their clothing for tailoring and we would be able to make some money to cover our expenses. Week one passed, and then week two: we did not get any customers. We realized this was not a good location for women's tailoring. We did not know what to do. Also, the sign was written in Dari, not in Pashto.

During this time, Agha-jan's siblings, who had left Afghanistan a few years before us in search of safety and found their way to Europe and the United States, heard from our relatives who lived in Pakistan that we just arrived with only one pair of clothes and had nothing to live with daily in Pakistan. One of them, who had not lived in Germany very long, immediately sent us some money to keep us going. That money again came at just the right time and kept our spirits up.

We bought much-needed supplies: cooking oil, flour, rice, and beans. We bought the largest bags we could to stock up, in case we had to move yet again. With the remaining money, we paid the rent and bought mattresses, blankets, and pillows.

The weather was getting cooler in Pakistan. People were getting ready for the winter. To us, it looked like spring, because there was no snow, no ice, and no cold breeze, just green nature.

The night before we bought all this stuff, we had only one blanket, the one Agha-jan wore when we left Kabul. He gave that blanket to me to use since we had become refugee. That night, while I was asleep, I heard a noise. It was not a cry, not a nightmare; it sounded different. I immediately woke up and saw that my father slept on one side and had his hands between his legs, and he was shaking. That sound was from cold; he was freezing as he slept. I immediately covered him with the blanket that I had while he was asleep. In the morning, we bought stronger clear plastic, to cover the windowless windows, blankets, and other necessary items.

Wow, we could cook food in our own dishes, sleep on our own mattresses, and have our own blankets! We would not freeze in the middle of the night again. The first day when I cooked in our own pot and pan, the smell of onions cooking in the oil brought me back to life; that smell made me hope again that we would have our own home, our own food and our own life.

That day, we began slowly building up a home again. In a short time, the family of the relative who came with us from Afghanistan, who currently lived in Islamabad,

Pakistan, sent us a couple old area rugs and a small black and white television. My heart was bursting with happiness! Day by day, I felt more secure.

We lived in that house for a couple months, until a dark cloud covered the Peshawar sky. Heavy rain began to fall and flooded our home. The plastic did not keep the heavy rain and wind out. Mud and water filled the room, and just like that, we were homeless yet again.

We packed up our belongings and set off to look for another home. Abdul and his family became our host again and let us stay with them until we could find a place. In a couple of days, we found a place in a better location and of much better construction. This time we rented a room from an Afghan family who we never met before; we became a tenant of a tenant. We immediately paid the first month's rent and moved in.

Again, Agha-jan hung his little sign "Women's Tailoring" on the door of our house.

The environment in our new neighborhood was different. A lot of Afghans who had left Afghanistan in recent years lived in the area.

In a few days, our first customer knocked on the door. In the coming days, Agha-jan received new customers every day. He was busy sewing women's clothing. Sewing was one of the skills he had learned when he was a child. As he grew, his skills improved, and he became a very successful professional tailor. He had previously used his skill mostly as a method of supplementing his income, but his side job in Afghanistan turned out to be our main source of income in Pakistan.

Since Agha-jan was busy with his new business and paying our expenses, I decided to enroll in an English class. Agha-jan encouraged me to enroll and paid my expenses.

Our life was starting to balance out and to feel more secure. Little by little, we were able to buy more household items and began looking for another home closer to Islamabad.

One day Agha-jan became sick again and was not able to work. Our relative living in Germany wrote and wished to pay our rent so that we could focus on getting our life back to normal. They wanted us to move to Islamabad and live in a house with her in-laws. Since we needed that support, we could not turn down that opportunity. We decided to move again. This time we were planning to change cities, moving from Peshawar to Islamabad. We packed and start moving the next day. My father's customers were not happy to see us leaving! He had, in a short time, gathered a great number of loyal customers.

We arrived in Islamabad, the capital of Pakistan. It was an early evening. Islamabad was a young city that had been built during the 1960's. With all its beauty, such as a forest boasting large trees and flowers everywhere, it fascinated me immediately.

Arriving in Islamabad, the car stopped in front of a two-storied house with a large iron gate. This was the house where we would live. The large rooms, with lots of large windows, were so alive and airy.

The beautiful granite floors were so clean, and the hallways seemed to go on forever. I wandered into the room we were to live in. It was the living room of that house, but we would use it as a living room, bedroom, family room and dining room. There was another family living on the same floor. They got the two bedrooms which were their living room, family room, dining room and bedrooms. We were lucky that we got the bigger room of the house. Oh my God, I was overjoyed, overwhelmed and very happy!

The neighbor gave us the tour, showing us the kitchen and bathrooms, which we would be sharing. We unpacked our meager but steadily growing household items and boxes.

In a few days, we were settled and ready to start the second phase of our new life.

Here, Agha-jan hung the tailoring sign on the house door. Even though he was still sick, he did not want to rely on others. But luck was not with him this time; he did not get any customers, even though there were a lot of Afghans living in that area.

Therefore, we became completely dependent on the relatives in Germany to send us money to pay our bills and expenses. Every month we waited for them to call us and tell us they had sent us the money. We knew that it was not easy for them to support us in Pakistan, but we did not have any other choice. They were our heroes. We did not know how long they could, and wanted to, do that.

One day a loved one told me there was a local school teaching Afghan children that had been displaced by the war. Hearing that, my eyes got big! I said "Really? I wonder if she would hire me as a teacher." With lots of confidence I said, "I can teach." That school was very close to our home, so the following day I visited the school to find out if they needed teachers.

It was a private Pakistani school. In the afternoon, they rented out space to Afghans to conduct classes. I went to the administration office to meet with the director of the school. I asked if they had any vacancies for a teacher. She said "No, today is the last day of school for the year. You can return in a few months to see if there would be any openings." I was so enthusiastic and started counting the days until the summer break ended and school would resume.

In August, I returned to meet again with the director. She said, "We have an opening for a substitute teacher to teach 9th grade!"

I was thrilled and immediately responded, "Yes, of course." We sat in her office and discussed the curriculum, school philosophy, student demographics, textbooks, and weekly planning. We toured the classrooms, and she introduced me to fellow teachers and students.

While we were touring the school, she received a message that the 'Dari' language teacher would not be able to come in today. She stopped and looked at me and said, "Would you be able to substitute for her?" She apologized for the imposition, but secretly this is what I needed to get my spirits flowing again. I was thrilled.

I followed the class schedules and entered the classroom. My heart happily jumped to be needed and busy. Boys and girls were in the same class. Some of them looked older for the 9th grade. They were quiet, trying to judge the new teacher.

When I opened the textbook, it reminded me of my own 9th grade. I began reading a poem on the first page and drew the students' attention to the words spoken before I translated it for them. Dari is one of the main languages in Afghanistan, but poems need to be translated into a non-poem until the audience knows what the poet's purpose was. The students began to become engaged in the poem. I started walking slowly around the classroom while I was reading and translating the poem. With each step, I felt more and more at home. The students were quiet. We went over the poem several times and slowly digested the meaning of the words. The students were following each word that I read and were very open to the text.

After I finished the first reading, I noticed the students raising their hands. In the Afghan education system, when a student raises his or her hand that means 'I have learned the lesson and I want to translate the text myself.' I was thrilled that the students felt secure with me and engaged.

From that day on I became a teacher. I never thought I would become a teacher one day. My goal was to become an engineer after graduating engineering college in Afghanistan. Sometimes you work toward one thing, and then God has a different plan for you.

Every day I worked hard to become a better and better teacher and an inspiration to my students.

For the past year, our relatives in Germany had supported us financially. They paid our rent, utility bills and food. I needed to find a way to provide for ourselves.

One day, a few students asked me if I could help them with their English after school. I agreed.

We met at home the next day after school. Students sat on the floor of my home for a couple of hours each day and learned English. This was some well needed additional income. I was very passionate about education for all Afghan kids, so I was very thorough and welcomed those who need my help.

At this time, more than two million Afghan refugees lived in Pakistan. There were lots of Afghan kids who were not able to pursue education because their families were not able to afford school fees, uniforms, and textbooks. Most children would have to work to put food on their families' dasterkhon, or tablecloth.

Many children between the ages of 5 and 17 worked as maids or servants or selling goods in the streets or at markets to support their family. Those young people had witnessed extreme violence and abuse during the ongoing fighting in Afghanistan and while escaping from their country and crossing the international borders.

Those children were the future of Afghanistan, a country that struggled, both culturally and politically, for generations. It was very clear that the people of Afghanistan had not only lost their homes, lives, wealth, and health; they had also lost their children's future. The future citizens of Afghanistan were facing streams of darkness by not being educated. What a dark future, what a dark life. I witnessed the Afghan children surviving in Pakistan. I could not even imagine the hardships that Afghan children were facing in our neighboring countries such as Iran, Tajikistan, Uzbekistan and India.

I wanted to do something to help those kids, but what and how? I asked myself, "How I can help them?" All these questions were like a storm in my mind that need to find its way out to destroy the despair and disappointment that had built up in people's hearts and to help them move toward a bright future. The beautiful Afghanistan and its people deserve to be happy; the people have the right to be educated.

That day, with all these thoughts and questions swirling in my brain, I wanted to share my ideas with Agha-jan and see what he thought. I went and sat by him on the Afghan mattress covered with a beautiful green cloth. I said, "Agha-jan, what if I open a school for Afghan children?"

He looked at me with a beautiful smile and said, "You can."

I thought he said that seriously. I continued talking. I said, "I am always thinking about opening a school for Afghan kids who are in danger of losing their school years."

I saw his beautiful smile change to a look of wonder. He said, "At first when you said that, I thought you were saying that you wish you could do that. But you sound serious." He said, "I understand you very well, but how can you do that? Do you know that it is not easy? We do not have money, and you are very young and do not have the experience to do all this work." He continued, "My daughter, I know that you are a hard worker, and I admire you for thinking about Afghan kids' future, but what you do now is a lot."

After a deep breath I said, "So, yes. What I do now is really little. I help kids who have money and are able to pay the school fee as well as a tutoring fee. But I really worry for kids who are not able to pay even the school fee. As a result, they end up not going to school. If I oversaw the Afghan schools here, I would charge a lower fee that would allow all these kids to attend school. How can a refugee family pay for their children's education, while they do not have money to buy them food and pay for their health care?"

As soon as I said that, my voice got so shaky. This was the first time I had talked about something like that. "Since I started teaching at the school, and I saw the Afghan refugee kids on streets deprived of education, this feeling has come alive in me to do something to help them. I kept this feeling in my heart for some time, and now it comes out."

Agha-jan said, "I see; it came out with a lot of pain that even effected your voice."

I was not crying, but there was someone inside me that was crying for the future of Afghan kids and Afghan society. I went on and on, with Agha-jan as my only audience.

After a pause he said, "I know that we have nothing in our hands to help those needy kids and their families, but our heart is full of hope. God is always great. Follow your thoughts; God will help you."

I was so happy after Agha-jan said that. I said, "Dad, I do not know, but I think something is on its way. What it will be, I do not know."

That day the idea of establishing a school filled my head. Then questions started. "I do not have any funds to cover the basics; how do I start? What happens if I fail?" That night, instead of sleeping, I was thinking, brain storming and planning in my head. "If I have a school, I would do this. I would do that." Lots of questions and worries started swirling in my brain. It was a long night; I lay awake with closed eyes. I was thinking and thinking and drawing a plan in my dreams of how and from where to start and what my first steps would be.

The next day, I went to the nearest Pakistani private school and met with the principal/founder. It was a small building with 6 classrooms, well equipped with school supplies. Their school ran from 8 a.m.to 12:00

noon, so in the afternoon the school building was not used. I asked them if they were willing to rent us the building from 12:00 PM to 7:00 PM Monday through Friday. I also explained that I was planning to start from scratch, with no funds, and that I hoped to get students with low fees to cover the expenses of school. The Pakistani principal and his wife agreed to not charge me any rent for the first month until I enrolled students.

Woohoo! Such a big achievement: finding a school that had six classrooms and a back yard that could be used as a couple classrooms, with first month rent- and utility- free. Wow! I immediately scheduled time to come back the next day and write the contract. What my next step would be, I did not know. Maybe advertise that a new school was opening for the Afghan refugee children, recruit teachers who could volunteer for a couple months, find books, and make plans … lots of things. I came home, my head full of dreams and plans, and shared the news with Agha-jan.

The next morning, I shared the news with my home school English class students. I also resigned from the school where I was teaching. I saw a lot of excitement in the class and almost everyone wanted to quit their school and join my school which was not up and running yet. I saw their happiness, their big smiles, and the joy in their beautiful eyes. I knew where their happiness came from. I knew they were hungry not only for education, but for support and care, too; and they knew they would get that under my leadership.

That day the class ended with a lot of questions like, "How this will work? What if I do this? And who will do that?" They were already taking ownership and wanting to be part of this big initiative.

The students left, and I went to review my plan to see what I needed to do today. But my door bell started ringing. Not a big surprise. It was a few students with their parents. I invited them in. In the Afghan culture, you must serve tea to visitors, so I did. The parents came to let me know that they wanted to support this initiative; as soon as the school opened, they would enroll their children in my school.

The afternoon of that day the news reached the neighboring schools. The next day, one of my teaching colleagues referred her sister, a college student in Afghanistan, to teach for free in the first couple of months. Wow! How did it happen? Who does all these things? It was God doing everything for us. I was a resource that God directed to go that route.
In a couple of days, the tenancy was signed with the Pakistani school owner, two teachers were hired, and the start date was determined. But still loads of work lay ahead of me: developing forms, class journal, class timetable, and books by levels. I needed to advertise for the grand opening. Choosing a name for the school, choosing student uniform colors, and lots more was waiting to be done.

Since my home-schooling name was Maiwand, after an historical place in Afghanistan, I named the school Maiwand school.

School began on a sunny afternoon. On the way to school, I saw our advertisements hanging on the walls, from one side of the street to the other. "Oh my God, please help me, and be with me and the people that support me and my father on this path," I prayed silently.

I arrived at school, went to the office, turned on the fan, put my purse on the principal's desk and sat on the chair. Looking around the office silently, I thought, "This is the office the Pakistani school uses during the morning. And in the afternoon, it is all ours." While I was walking in the land of my thoughts, I heard the voices of the young boys and girls who helped me hang all those advertisements and spread the word about opening the new school. They were at the office door waiting for me to tell them to come in. Each one of them looked great, happy and ready for a new start, dressed up for school with their backpacks. It was the first day.

Our school registration began. On the first day, I registered more than forty students for 1st, 2nd, 3rd, 4th, 5th and 6th grades. More than half came from neighboring schools, and the rest were kids that were having financial difficultly and were not able to go to school due to school's high fees.

Work began. I assigned subjects to teachers who had expertise in each area, completed school calendar planning, and set a high standard goal for achievement.

And now the first real challenge began to rear its head. The first payment was due in a month; we had only one month to collect enough fees to pay the school rent, utilities, and other costs. We needed more students. In order to achieve that, we had to work hard advertising to let people know about the discount program for families that were not able to afford school's high fees for their children.

The first couple of months were super busy with
registration. We were able to fill all six classes. Our 1st
grade filled very fast with lovely and beautiful kids.
It was heartbreaking to see some of our 1st grade kids
with broken sandals, with their notebooks and pens in a
plastic bag, and with poor hygiene. The only thing that
I could do to help was to not charge one of the kids if
there were more than three siblings.

More teachers were hired. Days went fast. I was busy.
I loved what I did; I spent all my energy and used all
my resources toward this initiative, because I knew that
whatever I did was not wasted. Someday it would pay
back to my country and its people.

Not long after school opened, one day on the way to
school, I noticed a few teen boys gathered at the corner
of the narrow road. It looked so strange to me, like they
were planning to attack someone. I was so scared; my
legs went weak, and I was so afraid to go forward. Then
I heard the voice of Agha-jan from behind me! He said,
"Do not be scared. I am behind you; keep going."

When I looked back, I saw that Agha-jan was coming,
with his friend who was an instructor at a Karate club.
As soon as the boys saw them, they started running
away. As we got closer to school, I saw that all our
advertisements and signs were destroyed. We arrived
at school, and I saw that the students from grade 6 who
had assisted with the grand opening were cleaning the
messages that were written on the door and wall of the
school. They were trying to clean them before I arrived.
They did not want me to see all the bad words
about me.

This was a warning from the Afghan neighboring schools. It sounded like the schools around me were not happy with me coming among them. They felt threatened, so they were trying to destroy all this effort and not let me continue my work. But I had to be strong and do the work and move forward.

This was the beginning of the journey. Those threats opened my eyes wide. I must tighten my belt in order to overcome the challenges that I would see on this path. Agha-jan had guessed about the threats. That is why he was prepared and watching me without letting me know.

This was a new challenge that I had not thought about before. The only thing we could do was to pray and ask God to protect us from any danger and help us to continue helping people who needed education. When I started this initiative, it was in my heart and my mind that I wanted to help, not to take away business from people who had schools or were running schools. Days went fast. Life was flying, and we were very busy in the first few months with enrollment, teaching, meeting with parents and so on.

Now, it was time to register the school with the Afghan school association that was recognized by the Afghan embassy in Pakistan, before the Taliban regime. For us to be a member of that organization, I had to write a request to join their membership. The benefit of having the membership was to provide a recognized document to students once they graduated. Once they returned to Afghanistan, if there was any peace and normal life in place, the degree would be accepted there.

I wrote the three-page long request. Agha-jan volunteered to deliver it and help with that process. The following day he left home hoping to come back with good news. We did not know what to expect. That day Agha-jan met with the board director and her deputy. Their response was not positive at first. They did not like the idea of having the third school in about two or three miles of each other.

Agha-jan got a "no" from them. But before he left, he told them, "Before I go, I want to let you know that at this time none of us can refer to any census data about how many Afghans live in that area and how many schools are needed there. Second, I want to let you know that there is no monitoring in the current schools to check how they teach. And third, our goal is not to take away anyone's business; our mission is to provide great and affordable education to Afghan refugee children who are the asset of our country in the future." He said that and start walking toward the door to leave. Both the director and her deputy stood up from their chairs and asked him to please wait and stay longer to discuss this request. They both admitted they were contacted by our neighborhood schools, who filed a complaint against us, saying this new school wanted to steal their students and run them out of businesses.

The director told Agha-jan, "After hearing your goal and your mission, I am impressed."

That day Agha-jan came home with good news. Our membership was accepted. We become a board member, and now our school had all the rights the other Afghan refugee schools had. A few days later, I received the schedule for the board meetings for the whole year. The next meeting was in couple days; I would have to attend.

Attending that meeting was very hard for me emotionally. I knew the school owners in my neighborhood did not like me and did not want to see me as their peer.

The day of the meeting, I woke up early and got ready to leave. Agha-jan prayed for me to be successful. I left the house with much fear of how people would treat me there. When I arrived at the Afghan Schools Association (ASA), the room was full of school founders, principals, and their assistants. I found a chair to sit at the big table in the conference room.

The meeting began, and they went around the table to introduce themselves. At my turn, before I introduced myself, I saw the two principals/founders from my area sitting next to each other and whispering, looking at me with very unhappy faces. I introduced myself as a new board member and the Maiwand school founder/principal. The two ladies raised their voices and said, "We wonder why she is here. This association is meant to be for existing schools and not for new schools."

The director said, "We invited her to attend this meeting as a board member. Any school that serves 100-plus students, with a mission to serve Afghan refugee children, will be part of us." They argued about the membership fees; the director informed them that it was paid for the past months.

Wow! A very stressful day fighting for the rights of my students. I came back bringing good news to Agha-jan and to the teachers and students: Save the Children would provide us a mobile library that students and teachers could use!

A month later we got visitors from ASA for a tour. A few months after that, our school participated in the annual celebration event through the ASA, where I received an award of appreciation. As these were all happening, our students increased to nearly 300. A few months later, I received my second award from the ASA.

With all that success and moving forward on that rewarding path, I still was no one; I did not know what would happen tomorrow.

I was among close to three million Afghan refugees in Pakistan, living in an uncertain situation. We did not know what would happen to us the next day. We lived in Pakistan with no legal documentation to live there, to work or to study. Of course, we did not have any rights. The Pakistani people were good to Afghans if they paid their rent on time and paid their share of utilities. The house owners in Pakistan were making good money from renting their houses or parts of their houses to Afghan refugees.

Decades of war and civil strife, as well as the Taliban regime, had made Afghans the world's largest refugee population. At that time, nearly three million Afghans resided in Pakistan. Their homes in Afghanistan had been destroyed. There was no education, no work, no health care system; and overall, there was no safe life. During the time, millions of Afghan women, men, and children missed years of schooling as refugees in Pakistan.

Even though the life of Afghan refugees in Pakistan was not good, the one good thing was that they spent their days and nights outside of a war and horror zone. Were they safe in Pakistan? Yes and no; there was no war, but we feared that any time the Pakistani government could send us back to Afghanistan.

A great hope replaced this fear for Agha-jan and me. I came home one Friday evening, after a busy day. As soon as I came in the door, Agha-jan said, "They just left."

"Who?"

He said, "Your auntie. She is wanting you to help them write a letter to an organization that assists refugees, sending them abroad for resettlement."

I said, "I would love to help, but why couldn't she stay longer, until I came?"

Agha-jan said, "She wanted to get home before it gets dark. Maybe she will come back tomorrow."

A couple weeks passed; we hadn't heard from her. We decide to go to her home and see if she still needed me to help her write that letter.

They lived in Islamabad city where it was so difficult for Afghans to navigate without any passport, especially for Afghan males. The Pakistani Police stopped them and charged them money. If they did not have money, jail was the only option.

Whenever we went to that part of town, Agha-jan had to be careful to not cross the Islamabad Police. Even with that fear, we still wanted to go help her. It was Sunday afternoon when we got there. She was very happy to see us. After drinking a few cups of

Afghan tea, my father told her why we were there. She said, "There was a rumor that there is an organization that sends Afghan women to other countries for resettlement." Auntie wanted to apply for that program and asked me to write a letter that explained her situation.

I said, "Sure. What is the name of that office?"

She said, "I do not know the name, but I know its location."

"For me to write a letter or request, I have to know who the audience is," I said.

Since she knew the location, she asked me to go with her and ask them in person. I told her we could go, but we may not be able to talk with them since it was Sunday and the offices would be closed.

So, we went. It was a few miles from their home, and when we arrived, of course the office was closed. Its big white and blue sign caught my eye immediately: United Nations High Commissioner for Refugees (UNHCR). I said, "Oh, it is UNHCR!" My heart told me we were in the right place. I love this organization and its mission.

We came home, and I told Agha-jan that it was the UNHCR office. I had read about UNHCR's mandate and primary purpose in a flyer not long before. I went on, explaining that the primary purpose of UNHCR is to safeguard the rights and well-being of refugees and to ensure that everyone can exercise the right to seek asylum and find safe refuge in another place, with the option to return home voluntarily, integrate locally or to resettle in a third country. I also told them about the humanitarian assistance that UNHCR provides to people in need; for example, the tents in refugee camps in Peshawar. This was all my knowledge about UNHCR back then.

We were all like birds, anxious to fly and arrive at a safe place and build a shelter.

"I hope it turns out to be right and this agency can help us," Aunt said.

"UNHCR is a trusted organization," I told her. "I want to apply for safety, too."

In a couple days, we found ourselves behind the UNHCR office door. There were people of other nationalities, like Iranians and Somalis. I went to the window and explained to the man who worked there that we heard this office was accepting applications for protection and sending people to other countries.

He said, "Yes, bring us your letter explaining why you need protection."

I came home and wrote my situation and explained why I was not able to return to Afghanistan.

The next day, as soon as I submitted my request, I received an appointment for an interview in a couple weeks.

The day of my interview I was so excited, worried and embarrassed. I had never been interviewed before and could not imagine what to expect. I was in the UNHCR's office, among lots of people from Afghanistan, Iran, Somalia and others, waiting to be called. The interviewer came out and called my name. I went in and sat on a chair across from his desk. He had my letter in his hands. He started asking questions, doing an extensive interview. Wow! A lot of why, when, how, who and what. It was extremely difficult for me to talk about what my family had been through. Since I trusted this organization, I told them about the war and its effect on my family in Afghanistan. At the end, he said that they would let me know by mail the result of the interview.

I headed home, my next step being to watch for the mail. On the way home, my head was full of thoughts. What would happen? Are they really helping people? Is this possible, sending people to other countries? I did not know.

Then my thoughts turned to daydreaming that Afghanistan was in peace again, no Taliban, no war, no fear. We would return home; I could go back to school and continue my education, become an engineer and play a big part in rebuilding my home and my hometown that was destroyed during the war. The noisy street in Islamabad did not let me continue with my daydreaming. A driver's head appeared from the window and, with a loud voice, said in Urdu, "Hey Afghani, walk careful!" I shook and suddenly came to myself. By the time I said sorry, the car was already gone.

It was a very hot summer day in Islamabad. I arrived at the crowded bus station in the city center and took the bus home. The buses in Pakistan ran with open windows, having no AC at that time. The hot wind blew while the bus navigated Islamabad's busy streets.

After 45 minutes, I arrived back in my part of the city. I got off the bus and walked down the busy alley. Shops such as a bakery, grocery, bicycle repairer and so on were on both sides of the narrow street. The sun was shining hard; what a hot day! I was thirsty, and my tongue was dry like a desert that has not seen water for years. As soon as I entered in the house, I ran to the kitchen, got a glass of water, leaned on the kitchen wall and drank.

That day looked different to me. I was a queen in my dreams and thoughts and was walking in a land I could not name. I had an interview. It was not like a test or a lesson. It was me, sitting in a chair and telling the interviewer about my history. I told myself that they would send me a letter. From now on I must wait for the post man every day. What would their letter tell me? It seemed so interesting. I hope it is not a game, I said. No, it is not; why would they fool people? No, he looked serious, but what will their letter say to us?

I spent the rest of the day thinking about the letter. That night I asked Agha-jan to go to Fahima's home and share the news with them. I wore my big scarf, and we left for Fahima's house. When she and her family saw us, they became very happy. But the happiness that we brought with us was different; it was from the bottom of our hearts; it had the freedom message; it had the safety message. We started talking. We told them about the opportunity. She was happy to hear about this and said that finally a door of hope is open for the Afghans that lost everything in Afghanistan and cannot return. That night I helped her write the request letter for protection to bring to the UNHCR tomorrow. I did not know what to expect after the first interview.

After a few interviews, UNHCR refers the refugee applicant to the United States (U.S.) for resettlement and processing by a Resettlement Support Center (RSC)[5], if that refugee is a chosen to be sent to the U.S. The RSCs prepare[6] eligible refugee applications for U.S. resettlement[7] consideration.

The total processing time varies depending on an applicant's location and other circumstances, but the average time from the initial UNHCR referral to arrival as a refugee in the United States is about 18-24 months.

We did not know anything about this process at that time. I thought the UNHCR office in Pakistan decided who is eligible for resettling in a third country and who is not eligible.

Seeking protection had not changed my vision and my action as far as my school initiative. At the time, my students reached nearly two hundred. The fee that was paid by students was spent on school rent, teachers' salaries and school supplies.

---

[5] The RSCs collect biographic and other information from the applicants to prepare for the adjudication interview and for security screening. Officers from the Department of Homeland Security's U.S. Citizenship and Immigration Services (USCIS) review all the information that the RSC has collected and also conduct an in-person interview with each refugee applicant before deciding whether to approve him or her for resettlement in the United States.

[6] After a refugee is approved by USCIS, they will send the refugees to complete a health screening to identify medical needs and to ensure that those with a contagious disease, such as tuberculosis, do not enter the United States. Finally, the RSC requests a "sponsorship assurance" from a U.S.-based resettlement agency that is experienced in helping newly arrived refugees. Most refugees undergo a brief U.S. cultural orientation course prior to departure for the United States.

[7] Those refugees who are approved by USCIS receive assistance upon arrival in the United States through the Department of State's Reception and Placement Program – a cooperative public-private program made up of several participants. The support of millions of Americans is fundamental to the program's success. Though Congress mandated the program, it is local communities that have ensured the success of the resettlement program by welcoming and helping refugees from around the world.

Agha-jan had been worried about me, my life, and our uncertain future. We were waiting anxiously for the result of our interviews with UNHCR; it had been more than a year since my third interview. One day, he told me to write another letter to UNHCR to follow up on the status of our interviews from a year ago.

At that time, UNHCR was the first to come to mind when the question of safety and protection arose. Of course, God is the first and last to ask for help; but at that moment, with direction from our God, UNHCR was our last resort to seek hope. We, like all other refugees, worried about our life and were always seeking a place to be safe. So, I wrote a letter which sounded a little complaining about the delay and about not communicating with us about the status of our application.

The next day, early in the morning, Agha-jan hand delivered the letter to the UNHCR office and dropped it in an application bag outside the office. It had been more than a year since the first time we went there. At that time, the process was very easy. You met a real person who accepted the application. But now, due to a high volume of applicants, you simply dropped your application in the application bag which was picked up by staff toward the end of each business day. Then God knows when they will read it and when they will get back to you.

Agha-jan came home and said that he dropped the letter to the big bag. He did not feel optimistic about that, since it was a different approach. He said, "Who know if they will read it?"

Two weeks later, I heard a motorcyclist ring our doorbell. Now a motorcyclist is not the regular post man. He had a letter for us from UNHCR, and he asked for a signature to acknowledge that I received the letter. Sure enough, it was an interview letter.

Agha-jan and I impatiently waited for the day of the interview. That day finally arrived. We took a taxi, and as soon as we arrived at the UNHCR office, we learned that we needed to be in a different location where I had never been before. We got another taxi and went to that location. This office was not as busy as the main one. They called my name, and both Agha-jan and I went in. The interviewer started asking us questions about who we were and why we requested protection. His questions were not new to us. I said, "Sorry, we already answered these questions before in the main office."

He said, "What? You have been interviewed with us before?" I said yes and provided him the letters and envelops that I got from my previous interviews. Then I explained that after a series of interviews, we had not heard from their office, and that is why we followed up: to see what the status of our application was.

After my explanation, the tone of the interview changed. He stopped the interview and went to copy all the documents that I provided him from my previous interviews. That was the end of my interview that day. He said, "We will notify you by mail about the next step."

Again, we left the office not knowing what would happen next. In a couple of days, I heard the doorbell rung by that motorcyclist again. We got another notice to come for an interview. Again, different location, different people. This was a very extensive interview, and at the end we learned that our application for protection was accepted. We could now resettle in a third country as refugees!

Wow! (Tears start coming even now as I remember that moment and am writing about it.) I could not believe it! Is it real? I kept asking myself. Are we going to be safe soon? Wow, I will have the right to study and work. I will live in freedom. Wow. I will not be afraid of my shadow again. I will have my rights.

Then my thoughts start comparing good hearts that are full of love and hard hearts that are hard as stone. I told myself, *Look at the world and its people. There are people in my country who seem to speak like me and claim to practice the same religion and same culture, but their hearts are like stone. They persecute millions of Afghans, steal their rights, and make them leave their homes and country. But on the other side of this beautiful world, there are people who think about you, who give you hope, share their home with you, let you be like them, advocate for your rights and give you the same rights as they have. Not only that, they pass a protection act in their constitution and open their hands to rescue you from danger and give you the right to live in freedom which everyone in this world deserves.*

I rubbed my eyes like I had woken up from a deep sleep. There was a huge happiness dancing inside me: we got approved! We got approved! A few days later, we attended a cultural orientation and went through a medical examination. Everything was new for us. During the cultural orientation we watched a video which walked us through how to find a job and how to adjust to your new life and to new hope. When we came to Pakistan, we had to figure out how to live, how to find a job and survive. Now some one guided us. I felt safe and supported from that moment on.

We were referred to the International Organization for Migration (IOM) office. I did not know what IOM stood for or what their job was. It was Tuesday afternoon. I, with Fahima, who was for me as an older sister, and her husband, went to IOM to see what the next step was. As soon as I got there, I spoke with the person at the front desk. He let me in, and we went to a conference room. I sat on a chair at a big table. A couple women were there, too, before me, seemingly for the same reason I was there. In a few minutes, he came back with some papers. He gave me one of those and told me that our flight was scheduled for this date. As soon as I heard "flight," I was shocked.

I waited for him to finish talking, and then I bombarded him with questions: "Did I hear flight? Is this right? Where are they sending us? Who pays for our travel? When we are leaving?" His eyes got bigger and bigger. I thought he would yell at me to stop!

He very nicely said, "Sure, here are the details. You guys need to arrive at the airport on …. Bring your clothes with you. We will meet you there and will give you a bag that contains your documents. Do not open the bag. When you reach the U.S., give it to the officer there." He repeated that a few times: "Do not open the bag." We understood that, but I was so curious to know why we were not allowed to open the bag. Then we went over our flight information. From Islamabad to Karachi, Pakistan; from Karachi to Dubai, United Arab Emirates; from Dubai to Zurich, Switzerland; from Zurich to France; then to New York, the beautiful city of the U.S.; after that to Dallas, Texas; and our final destination was Phoenix, AZ.

Wow, I never had that kind of travel before! Then I asked, "How will we travel without a passport?"

He said, "Bring this paper with you to the airport. This is your ticket." He did not answer my question about the passport.

I left the IOM office and returned to the taxi where Fahima and her husband were waiting for me. I sat in the back seat and told them that we were leaving in five days. They looked at each other. Fahima's husband said, "Leaving?" They were not sure whether to believe me or not. They thought I was joking. I showed them the flight information. It was news to them. Fahima smiled and said, "Really? Really, in five days?" It was a big shock for them. Tears started coming from her eyes. She dried her tears with the side of her white scarf. Her tears told the story of separation, the story of pain and living lonely, the story of who we are. The questions: where we will go, what we will do, and how we will live? Who would we laugh with, who would we cry with, and who could we trust? And would there be a day when we would meet each other again?

Fahima was still waiting for a respond from UNHCR. They had their first interview; but after that, they were never called.

We arrived home with our big news: protection, safety, rights. We had been approved to resettle in a third country. They would send us to America (USA). Where in the USA? Phoenix. I had read about Arizona and the Grand Canyon in my English book, but I did not remember reading about its climate. I always thought America had cold and freezing weather.

The next day, Agha-jan went to the tailor shop and ordered a couple suits for himself. Ever since the Mujahideen took over the government of Afghanistan and our migration to Pakistan, Agha-jan had not worn suits. He had to wear that Afghan old style of clothes for men, since it was common in Pakistan. This told me that he missed who he was when he worked back home. I started sorting out our household items, things to sell, things to give away. Since we did not have that many household items, it took me only a couple days to do that. Now, I had to get clothes that I could wear in America. Since the fall of the communist regime in Afghanistan, I had not worn pants, skirts or short dresses.

I went to the tailor shop and picked some cloth in a dark gray color. I also picked a very beautiful design; the suit looked so good on the model.

In a couple days, I picked up my new clothes from the tailor shop. They looked beautiful to me. It had been a long time since I had worn business clothes. All I wore was the long, bigger size clothes that were covered with the big scarf. Or in Pakistan, I mostly wore Panjabi clothes composed of a dress that goes around the knees, pants that usually match the dress color and a long, big scarf.

The night before our flight, we packed our luggage: a couple Panjabis, the suit and a pair of sandals for me; a couple suits, pants and shirts for my Agha-jan; a blood pressure monitor for my father; our holy book (Quran), a Hafiz book, and a couple English dictionary books.

That luggage looked so big to me! I was so afraid to be overweight; on the other hand, we did not know how much we could take.

Finally, the day that changed my life arrived. We needed to be at the Islamabad International Airport by 4:00 PM. Agha-jan and I left the house for the airport. Fahima, her husband and her two little daughters came with us to the airport. As soon as we arrived, I saw a few families waiting there, people I had seen at the UNHCR office or at the IOM office or when we did the medical checkup. We went to stand with them. They were sitting quietly, all looking stressed out and embarrassed. We all were outside of the terminal. We did not know the next steps. A white car arrived and stopped at the curb. A couple Pakistani guys got out and came toward us. They had a bunch of big white plastic bags that had the IOM logo on them. So, it is real, I said to myself. I went through the whole process, but for some reason, I was on and off as far as believing it.

As soon as they reached us, they start calling out names and giving people their bags. This was the bag that we were not supposed to open. We got our bag. It was time to say goodbye to Suryia and her family in Pakistan. It was very hard. I felt we were slowly separating farther and farther from my home, my family, my country, my culture, my past and my history. I would never forget when her four-year- old daughter gave me her five rupee and told me to buy something to eat on the way to the U.S. I took her five rupee, and I could not look into her beautiful eyes full of tears. She did not want us to go, but we had no choice.

Then Agha-jan and I lined up to enter the terminal. There was a Pakistani police officer at the gate greeting us and telling us to enjoy our life in the U.S. This was the first time in Pakistan that we were not afraid walking by an officer.

We went through all those security check points at the airport and were finally seated on the airplane. This was my third time flying in my life. The first and second time I flew from Kunduz Provence to Kabul and back when I was a child. It was during the communist regime in Afghanistan. Ground transportation was not safe, so we traveled to Kabul to visit my grandmother, my aunts, my uncles and their children by airplane.

It was evening, and our plane was ready to depart. Such a lovely experience. Bye, Afghanistan; bye, Pakistan. Bye, uncertainty; bye, unsafety; bye, fear. Bye, danger; bye, hardship; bye, hopeless; and bye, nightmares! I said bye to all of those things, but I was not sure what we would find or see after we reached our final destination.

My hope was to never experience horror, fear, and sorrow again. My hope was to be safe and have my rights as a human being. And my hope was that all my dreams would come true. I knew that I might not be able to return to my country again under that government and regime. I couldn't find my family members that I had lost during the war in Afghanistan. I wouldn't see my home again. And finally, I would never get back any of those things that I lost or left behind. They will remain in my heart, in my memories and in my dreams. But now I needed to be alive while I was moving forward in this journey.

After a few hours, our plane landed in Karachi at night. The only thing I saw from the airplane window was the city lights. The IOM staff who traveled with us from Islamabad connected us with another big group of people, mostly women and children, who came from Kohita, another city of Pakistan. We all lined up again to get another plane to Dubai.

This was the longest journey for me and Agha-jan.

CHAPTER FIVE

Life in the United States

Arriving

After 24 hours, we arrived in Dallas to get our final flight to Phoenix. Dallas terminal was so big, like other terminals where we changed planes during this journey. But in Dallas, we were alone. The group of Afghan people we arrived with went to different states as soon as we got to JFK airport.

The IOM staff were assisting new arrivals get to their connecting flight for their destinations. So, Agha-jan and I were assigned to Phoenix as a "free case." Alone in Dallas, I had to find the gate for our next flight to Phoenix, so I asked a police officer in the Dallas airport, "Where can I find the gate for my next flight?"

With a smile, he said, "Sure, where are you going?"

I said, "Foniks."

With his smiling face, he asked, "Phoenix?"

"Yes."

He started walking and asked us to follow him. We arrived at the gate where our final flight was waiting for us. I think his big smile was about the way I pronounced "Phoenix" (Foniks). Or it could be because I had not told him where we are going; I just asked him where I could find the gate for our next flight.

One thing that you immediately notice is the people's attitudes and customer service in the U.S. Very nice and friendly. People looked very pleasant to me: the police officer, the flight attendants, people at the airport. People looked at us with a smile. They said hi, even though they did not know us. They said excuse me. Wow, lots of beauty in people's communication. In Pakistan and Afghanistan, this was not the case. If you smile at someone, specially of a different gender, people took that negatively. Or if you look at someone's eyes while talking, that's rude in Afghan culture.

So here in the U.S., from the first moment, we got culture shock. People smile at each other; people help each other; you can ask for help.

We got our seats on the last plane. As I looked out the window, the ground lights came on. "This is the second night, and we are still on our journey," I told my Agha-jan.

He said, "Yes, but the day and night are different between the U.S. and Asia." He said, "When I was a child, the U.S. assisted Afghanistan with some clothing and food items, like bags of flour to make bread. At that time in Afghanistan, we did not have white flour. Our flour was just wheat color. The bread from that white flour looked and tasted so strange to us. As a kid I wanted to know where America was, so I asked my older brother. He told me about the shape of the globe and explained that America is on the other side of this globe from us. I started thinking that people live on the other side of the ground where I am standing."

While Agha-jan was telling me about his childhood limited knowledge about the world, a woman in hejab came and put her backpack on the seat next to me. She sat down and fastened her seatbelt. Then she looked at me and asked, "What is the purpose of your trip to Phoenix?"

I did not understand what she meant. I said, "This is my first time going to Phoenix. We came as refugees, and my destination is Phoenix."

She said, "Oh, they're sending you guys to a desert."

I did not say anything to her, but as soon as I heard a desert, I started worrying. I was asking myself how we would live in a desert. Maybe they brought us here to build their desert. I looked at the darkness of the night from the plane window, with all these thoughts on my mind. After a couple hours, I saw the soft glow of the city lights on the ground appear. The plane started getting closer to the ground, and as it got closer, the beauty of the city appeared through those lights. The pilot announced that we were landing at the Sky Harbor Airport, Phoenix, Arizona. Wow, it does not look like a desert! It is a city, a big city, I said to myself. It was 10 pm, and the Phoenix terminal looked less busy than the other terminals that we had been through.

We were extremely tired. We left the plane, not knowing what to expect. As soon as we stepped out of the gate, someone called our last name and came toward us. Again, another pleasant person. He welcomed us to Arizona and said that he represented the resettlement agency and was here to take us to our apartment. This was not so strange to me, because I had read this in the Welcome to the United States book that I got during my cultural orientation in Pakistan. It explained the responsibility of the resettlement agencies, case managers, short term services, employment, transportation, education and more. So, after seeing him, I felt safe and explained to Agha-jan that he was from the resettlement agency and was here to help us.

We walked to the baggage area. Our baggage arrived, two small bags. He said, "Is that it?" I said yes. He did not let me carry the luggage. He helped us carry them to the car. In order to get to the car, we had to walk from the terminal to the garage outside of the terminal. As soon as we stepped outside the terminal building, I thought there was a heat fan somewhere. For a second, I looked around, and then I realized it was not a heat fan! It was the weather! This was the first time I experienced Arizona's weather. Warmer than Pakistan, the weather was very different than my expectation. It was hot! To me it felt like we were walking in a sauna. For that moment, I forgot about my goal to be safe. I said to myself, Oh God, I was so tired of hot weather in Pakistan and now you brought me to a hotter place!

I told Agha-jan, "I thought we said goodbye to the heat for ever, but it seems that no, the heat followed us, or we followed the heat."

Agha-jan said, "It looks like here is hotter than Pakistan because in September it starts cooling down there, but here it is still very hot."

I said, "Yes, even during the night!" Wow.

We arrived where the agency car was parked, and my father sat in the front seat. Just before we departed, he opened the window and offered a cigarette to the case manager. He said, "No thank you; I don't smoke." Agha-jan got his lighter to light his cigarette in the car. The case manager said, "Sorry sir, you are not allowed to smoke in the car."

Agha-jan looked him and thought he was joking. The case manager repeated, "We do not smoke in the car here. Even in our homes, you cannot smoke inside." Agha-jan was not happy to hear this! He rolled the window up and put his cigarette in his pocket.

We left the airport and merged onto the fast highways of Phoenix. The freeways looked scary to me because I had never ridden on such fast streets. Cars were driving so fast, with their windows closed.

The city looked like a different world to me. Hardly anyone was on the street. From the airport to the apartment, I was shocked, culture shocked; maybe scared a lot. A very strange feeling. I could not think; my mind was frozen. How would we live here? Agha-jan and I did not know anyone. The case manager who was driving turned his head a couple of times toward the back or over his shoulder while he was driving. I was sitting in the back seat, and I thought that he was looking at me, adding to my fear. Why was he looking at me? He should do his work and pay attention to driving. I learned a couple months later, when I took driving school, to look over your shoulder while you are changing lanes. He was not looking at me; he was driving safely and want to make sure there was no car in the next lane before he changed lanes. Of course, this was a culture shock to me. I came from a country where the women do not feel safe around men other than their father, brother, son or husband.

When we arrived at the apartment, the parking lot was dark and scary. As soon as the case manager opened the apartment door for us, we saw the living room. There was no hallway. Where we should put our shoes? No light at the ceiling, but there was a lamp at the side of the wall. We slowly took it all in. There were two beds, one love seat, and one dining table with two chairs. The refrigerator was full of food from meat to vegetable to dairy. There were a few dishes, and some pots and pans in their boxes, but I did not see a teapot. Afghans with no teapot. We were so tired and just wanted to go to bed and sleep.

The case manager gave us the key and told us he'd be back tomorrow morning to take us to apply for some important documents. He did not say what documents. He left.

As soon as he left, I unwrapped a blanket and pillow from their plastic packaging and jumped on the love seat - which was short for me to sleep on - and went to sleep. I do not remember where Agha-jan slept. The apartment was not set up as a welcoming home. The mattresses were standing against the living room wall, the box springs were sitting in the bedroom, the bed frames needed to be assembled; they were on the other wall near the mattress. That resettlement agency had only one employee who set up apartments in those days. He was overwhelmed setting up apartments because of the high volume of arrivals.

Our first night in America.

Early next morning, I woke up to the songs of birds sitting in a tree outside our window.

The window was covered with white blinds; I did not know how to open them. It was the first time I had seen that kind of window covering. Back home, we used cloth curtains to cover the windows. I found my way to the window glass through the blinds and saw outside. Wow! A swimming pool, green landscape, palm trees. Birds were in the tree. There was blue sky with lovely sunshine and clean air. Wow, everything looked gorgeous to me outside of my apartment. Then I started checking out the things inside our apartment.

Everything looked different, like the way the window opened by sliding to the side vs. in Afghanistan where our windows were designed differently. Like the carpet on the floor; back home we used big area rugs to cover the floor. The wooden walls; back home our homes were built with bricks, cement and stones; or in the country side, they build homes with mud or clay The kitchen inside faced the living room. The entry door opened from the living room right to the outside. What a strange place, but clean, lovely, and beautiful, I said. I went to the bathroom. It was kind of similar to our bathroom in Afghanistan: bathtub and shower, sink and toilet was not new to me.

I walked to the entrance door, and as I opened it, there again was beautiful sunshine, a clean parking lot, and newly mowed grass in front of the apartment. There was no one around. So quiet, very calm.

I closed the door, turned back to the living room, and sat in one of the two chairs at the dining table the agency had provided.

My first day in the U.S.

I said to myself, *This is my destination. I must start from zero.*

But, is this the zero point? No, it is not the zero point. I know what zero means, and how it looks and how it sounds and how it feels. When we first arrived in Pakistan and did not know where to go, THAT should be called the zero point, not this.

I repeated, *This is not the zero point.* On the first day, we have an apartment with its rent paid; it is furnished with necessities, and we have food. So I am not starting from zero.

That morning, my eyes were busy seeing all these new things, and my brain was busy analyzing all these differences and coming up with lots of but's, if's, what's, and how's. My brain started asking me questions which were not new to me, and I was so tired of hearing them. Questions for which I had no answer. *Am I still safe here? Do I have to escape again?* This time my brain answered its own questions. *No, I do not have to escape again. I am safe here. I am in America, where I have my rights as a human being.* Finally, I had arrived in a land that values people, values human beings, and values life.

CHAPTER SIX

Adjusting

I had reached another chapter in my life. My first day in the land of opportunity; my first day in the state of the Grand Canyon; my first day in the land of sun and brightness.

I felt that I was a different person. I had to learn the new life and work hard to get to my new hope. That was not easy. I had to start from somewhere.

At first, life in the U.S. was different substantially for me, in a lot of aspects, than my life in Afghanistan or Pakistan. Adjusting to the U.S. system and culture was so challenging and stressful.

In the first month after my arrival, I learned that I was the head of the household because I was employable. That was overwhelming news to me, because back home and even in Pakistan I was dependent on my Agha-jan. While it was true that I had started working in Pakistan, I still never thought that he was aging. Agha-jan went through a lot in Afghanistan; he lost everything. He was physically and emotionally injured.

But still, in Pakistan he tried to work to support me. He, my hero, had finally reached a land that took his hand and give him all his rights. Wow, such a wonderful system. People have their rights here.

I became so interested in learning the U.S. system and culture. To do that, I had to come up with a plan to guide me through the process. I came up with a list to focus on first. I had to improve my English to communicate better. I needed to learn about health insurance and medical appointments in order to help Agha-jan to navigate the health care system. I had to learn the housing laws and regulations, the traffic laws, work culture…. My list went on and on and on.

What I learned in this chapter of my life was that when you are new to a system and culture, you learn things partially, only enough to take you from point A to point B. This does not mean that people do not want to learn or are not interested in learning fully about that new system and culture. But in order move on, they have to keep pace with all other aspects of life that are priorities to them and to their families. The U.S. system and culture is huge! For a person who comes as a refugee to learn all of that within a few years is not possible.

People say the first few months after a refugee's arrival in the U.S. is a honeymoon stage for them. After that time, they face the reality that they must work and support their family. I do not know what people base that statement on. In my situation, I never felt that way. From the first day of my arrival in the U.S., I felt responsible for my life and my Agha-jan's life. I was worried all the time and looking for ways to succeed. Maybe people use the word "honeymoon" because of the rental and nutrition assistance that the government provides for refugees for a couple months. But to me it was not a honeymoon; it was a heavy load on my shoulders, and I was trying to find ways to relieve that heavy load. From the first day after my arrival, I was thinking about how to find a job, to earn income to pay for my expenses. This was my short-term goal.

Since I knew enough English to communicate, I started helping Afghans who were new arrivals and lived in the same apartment complex as we did. I read and translated their mail and communicated with their case managers, employment specialist, the apartment manager, and so on. That volunteer interpretation and translation was not only helping my neighbors who were from my country; it was also improving my knowledge and understanding about different services and programs.

Transportation was a big challenge for us. We had to rely on public transportation. In a big city, not knowing the address and using public transportation was so difficult for me. For example, when we wanted to buy some groceries, we had to walk to the bus station, wait for the bus to arrive, then take the bus for a couple miles to reach the grocery store. In Pakistan, this was not the case. The grocery store was down the road by my house. Everything was so accessible in Pakistan and Afghanistan. But here, we had to walk a few miles or take the bus to reach to a shop. The bus schedule was another issue - sometimes we waited for an hour at a bus stop to take the bus.

It was so difficult for me to adjust to the public transportation system. I had to move fast and make good use of every minute of the day. Waiting hours in a bus stop made me so impatient. So, in order to overcome this challenge or barrier, I had to learn driving, get my drivers license and buy a car.

At the same the time, I had to find a job, manage our monthly expenses and learn how to live in the U.S.

All of those were loads of stress on my mind. I did not know from where to start. The limited rental assistance from the agency was coming to its end, and I had to find a job before it ran out.

It was a beautiful day. I was admiring the green landscaping from our apartment window when I heard someone knocking on our door. As soon as I opened the door, I saw our neighbor who was from Bosnia and had come as a refugee a few months before us. He and his wife were very nice people. We were using their home phone to communicate with the agency case manager. That day he had come to tell me my case manager was on the phone. Whenever the case manager called us, it was something important. I thanked the neighbor and rushed to his apartment to answer the phone.

I picked up the phone and started speaking with case manager, trying to catch my breath from running the stairs. He told me our SS cards had arrived, and he wanted Agha-jan and me to go to the office and pick them up.

So, again we had to get a bus to get to the office. It took us three hours.

I received our SS cards. The case manager explained that with this document I could work, I could open a bank account, I could get a drivers license and lots more. He also told me to keep it in a safe place.

While we are talking with him, his supervisor came into his office and, with a very beautiful smile, greeted us. She sat next to me, gave me a one-page form, and told me to fill it out. She smiled and said, "I'll come back in a few minutes to take it from you." I did not know what the form was or why I should fill it out.

The case manager said, "Do not refuse it; it is a job offer." I still did not understand, so he explained. "She wants to hire you as an on-call interpreter." While we were still talking, she came back and stood by the door, and with a smiling face said, "You are already doing this work as a volunteer. We want to pay for the work you do. This is our job application."

Agha-jan and I were so happy to hear this. I said, "Sure! I want to work here!" I did not know that volunteer work counts. I immediately filled out the job application and got hired as an on-call interpreter. This was a great opportunity that came my way. I was so happy, plus shocked. That day I was hired as an interpreter. My first job in the U.S. started from that very day.

And now, how was I supposed to come to the work site? Using public transportation was the only option for me.

That evening, a couple from the Afghan community visited us. They arrived a few years before us and now wanted to give back and help a new arrival from their country. I shared with them about the transportation issue. They told us their stories about when they first came and advised me to get my driver's license as soon as possible and then get a car.

They said this is the first step to success. A few days later, I found my way to the DMV to get my driving permit. Then with the help of a couple women from the Afghan community, I started to learn to drive at a church parking lot. I will never forget their generosity for the time they spent with me, teaching me driving and allowing me to use their car to learn.

After a few driving lessons with the Afghan women, I ended up in a driving school and took a few driving classes. The first day of my driving lesson, the instructor came to pick me up from my apartment. Both Agha-jan and I were ready and started to get in his car. He told Agha-jan that he was not allowed to be in a student driving car. Agha-jan got so upset to hear that; it was so hard for him to allow me to be in a car with a stranger. The instructor further explained that he respects our culture, but he had to follow their company policy. Even though it was hard for Agha-jan to accept, he let me go take the driving classes.

This was the first time I drove on the road with an instructor next to me. I was so afraid and so careful; I looked straight ahead and did not want to blink my eyes while I was driving. After a few sessions, we went to the DMV to get the road test. I passed! Wow! I could not believe I had passed that test and got my driver's license. The instructor let me drive back to my home. He congratulated me and wished me safe driving.

I came home with very good news. I had driver's license, but no car. my father and I began thinking about buying a car. It was a good idea, but with no money, how could we buy a car?

At this time, more Afghan families were coming as refugees, and the agency had to provide them culturally and linguistically meaningful services. To do that, they had to call me to translate for them. I became very busy. Though my job was on-call, every day I had to meet the clients and the agency staff, either at the client's home or at the office, and accompany them to their appointments to help them with translation. There were weeks that I worked more than 40 hours.

In a couple of months, we were able to save some money to buy a car. My first car. With the help of the Afghan community members who were in the U.S. for many years, we found a used car that cost $3,000. The money that we had saved was not enough to cover that cost. We had to borrow some from another Afghan community member, who became Agha-jan's friend, and add it to our money to be able to purchase the car. The car was in very good condition, a red Geo Prizm.

Wow, a lot of changes in a few months in a new country! We were so happy. We had a camera, and were using that to capture our happiness and memories. My pictures were taken at an escalator, with a tall building, in parks, in my car with the door open, by the pool. We were enjoying every minute. I had a job and a car, and every day I came across something new. Agha-jan was receiving Social Security Income benefits and medical assistance. What a great life. Now that I am writing this book, it has been almost 20 years that I have lived in the U.S. I wish I could go back and live those days again. I miss those moments. I was like a baby who sees everything for the first time and wants to grab it or who is sometimes afraid to touch things, just watching but not wanting to get closer. The city life was not new to us, but life in the U.S. was. Even though I was born and raised in an educated family and lived a modern life in my country, life in the U.S. was way different. The system was very different than our life in Afghanistan.

I never drove in Afghanistan. I did not even know how to ride a bike. But as soon as I arrived in the U.S., I learned that driving skills are such an important aspect of life that everyone must have them.

The first day when I drove my car – hooo! It was very difficult! I had to go to work. On one hand I was very happy to have a car and not have to wait for a bus; on the other hand, I was so scared about how I would drive without an instructor.

That day, I left our apartment for work. After securing my seat belt and checking my mirror, I started the car and left the parking lot. I did good on the street - until I reached an intersection to turn left. The light turned green. Cars started coming from the opposite direction. The light turned yellow; the cars were still coming from the opposite direction and rushing to pass the intersection before it got red. I wanted to turn left, but the cars kept coming and would not let me. The light turned red on me while I was still in the middle of the intersection. Cars from the other side of the intersection let me turn left, but they were very angry at me. A couple people honked their horn at me to turn fast. I was so scared; my hands and feet were so cold and shaking. I turned left and started driving the busy street toward my office. All morning at work, in the back of my mind I was thinking about how to drive back home.

The clock hands reached 12:00 PM, and people started coming out of their offices. Some left the building, and some went to the kitchen. I smelled the food. A colleague came and saw me sitting at my desk. He said it was lunch time. I thought he was going to tell me where the lunch was served. But he did not say that. Instead, he said, "Did you bring lunch or do you want to grab something from outside?" This was so new to me! When he said this, I immediately understood that employees are responsible for their own lunch. Since I did not bring any lunch with me, and I did not have any money with me to buy lunch, I said, "Thank you; today I am fasting."

He said, "Oh ok."

In Afghanistan, at the time Agha-jan was employed, he did not have to bring his lunch to work. Companies had to provide free lunch for their employees, and some companies even provided free transportation. Wow, to me it looked so strange.

So, lunch time was over, and I was "fasting." In the afternoon, I had to provide translation assistance to an Afghan family who was scheduled for an employment orientation. It was a family of seven - husband, wife and five children. The case manager started asking them questions about their employment history in order to complete an employment plan. The husband said that in Afghanistan he worked as a cook. His wife never worked outside of the home. Then he asked me to tell the case manager to hire him as a cook in this office, the refugee resettlement agency. Before I translated this to the case manager, I told him, "They do not cook for their employees. Everyone brings food from home."

He looked at me strangely and said, "Really?"

I said, "Yes, today I learned that!" The case manager wanted to hear what we were talking about. I translated our conversation.

He laughed and said, "Oh, no we do not cook for our employees. That would be nice, ha?"

The day came to its end, and I left the office. At the parking lot, as soon as I saw my red car, I thanked God for everything that he gave me.

Again, driving fear: I had to drive from work to home during rush hour. The sky was cloudy, and rain started to fall. As soon as I left the parking lot, I saw the street was wet. I remembered that the Afghan women who taught me driving said to be careful when you drive when it rains, because the streets become slippery when you push the brake. With that in mind, I drove very slowly. I was driving ok, but people were honking and honking at me. My God, why are they doing that? Why are they mad at me again? I wondered. I knew the reason as soon as I become comfortable driving! I was driving very slowly, and the other cars wanted me to drive according the street speed limit.

A couple months later, I was hired as a full-time case manager within the same organization and then got promoted to the employment specialist/job developer/ matching grant coordinator. I worked for them for 9 years.

Our first year in the U.S. went very fast. I had a lot of energy, enthusiasm and eagerness to learn the new system and the new culture and to improve my language skills. During this time, I assisted other refugees from Afghanistan, Iran, Sudan, Iraq, Eretria,

Somalia, and more who were on the path to self-sufficiency. On top of all these heavy responsibilities and hard work, I had to be an Afghan girl. As soon as I came home, I went to the kitchen and started cooking Afghan food, then did cleaning and took care of my lovely Agha-jan. I wanted to be a good friend to the Afghan girls who came as refugees and lived with us in the same apartment complex. This friendship built an atmosphere for me that meant Agha-jan and I were not alone. We are still among those who understood us, who spoke like us, who ate the same kind of food, and finally, who shared the same culture. Being close to the Afghan community made me feel supported. As the Afghan famous poet Jalal al- Din Rumi (1207-1273) says:

> "Listen to the story told by the reed,
> of being separated.
> Since I was cut from the reedbed,
> I have made this crying sound.
> Anyone apart from someone he
> loves understands what I say.
> Anyone pulled from a source
> longs to go back.
> At any gathering I am there,
> mingling in the laughing and grieving."

As days went by, we met more and more people from the Afghan community, people who came in 1980s and were already settled. The couple Afghan women who helped me with driving were among those people. Other Afghan people had come as refugees after we arrived. In a few years we made a lot of friends from the Afghan community. We celebrated our traditional holidays with them as we would have with our family back home.

One of those holidays is Eid, the three-day celebration at the end of Ramadan fasting. Children receive gifts, money and sweets from their elders. Family and friends take time to visit, especially those they don't often see during the year. Afghans clean and cook and bake for days in preparation for this festive time of visiting one another. Agha-jan was a very respected person among them. Therefore, during Eid days, we had lots of visitors. It is part of Afghan culture that on the first day of the Eid, the younger people must visit the elders first, and the elders are waiting for the younger to come and visit them. Agha-jan loved Eid days! On Eid's first day, he dressed up in his lovely suit and tie. He was very nice looking anyway, but on Eid days he looked even nicer.

For me and some other Afghan people who worked, it was not easy to take time off from work to celebrate the three days of the Eid, and to spend all day cooking and serving food and tea to the visitors. Then I had to visit the people who visited my Agha-jan, to show them a return respect. Even without the traditional campfires late into the night, it was a very, very busy three days. It was too much for me, and at the end of the day I was completely drained of energy and vitality.

As time passed and we lived in the U.S. longer, we got to know more Afghans who lived in our city. We used to meet them on special occasions, such as Eid days, wedding parties, engagement parties, birthday parties, graduation parties and a few other religious and cultural events, such as Nowruz, the Persian New Year. Nowruz is the first day of the new year, March 21.

Nowruz is another big day for Afghans. Wherever they are, they celebrate Nowruz. It is not only our new year day, but it reminds us of our ancient history and culture, who we are, and where we came from. The celebration traditions include special food dishes, ceremonies, and games. One of the sweet dishes, Samanak, is made from germinated wheat and is cooked all night the eve of Nowruz. The women traditionally cook this together and have a special song they sing in the process. Nowruz is one of my favorite holidays. I said holiday, but it is only a holiday back home. Here I must work during Nowruz; or if I want to stay home, I must take the day off.

From childhood, Nowruz was a very special day for me. I remember when my mother started preparing for Nowruz a couple weeks before. She cleaned the house, made new clothes for us, cooked delicious food, and made Haft mewa (a fruit salad of seven different fruits). Agha-jan bought us school supplies and school uniforms which mentally prepared us for school to start the next day after Nowruz, which is the first day of the new year.

Since we left Afghanistan and became refugee, I did not use the Afghan calendar, the Shamsi Hijri calendar. This calendar is based on astronomy. The months corelate to the Zodiac signs, and the New Year always starts on the spring equinox. I did not need this calendar, since my work depended on the U.S. calendar. But for Agha-jan, it was not easy to make that change. Even though we did not need the Afghan calendar, Agha-jan always asked people who traveled back home to bring him the Afghan calendar.

When I talk about the Afghan calendar, it reminds me of the beauty of each season back home. Lovely spring, with its soft breeze; young, fresh green grass everywhere; apple and cherry trees with their white blossoms. The atmosphere was full of spring smells. Spring is a season of beginning and growth in Afghanistan. It is the beginning of the school year, and it is the planting season.

Then summer, a season of harvest. It was the time of the year to eat delicious melon and watermelon, grapes all kinds and all other fruits and vegetables.
During our first days in the U.S., every fruit and vegetable tested different to us. I could not find the natural sweetness of each fruit or vegetable here.
One day Agha-jan went with his friend to a grocery store and bought some fruits. As soon as I started unpacking the groceries he brought, the peaches smelled and looked appealing to me. I immediately washed one of them and started eating.

Wow! As soon as I took the first bite, my eyes got big. I said to myself, it is the same. Yes, it is like our peaches. Yes, it was very delicious and tasted like peaches from my country. I asked Agha-jan where they bought these fruits. He said, "Tomorrow we can go back to that store and buy more." Sure enough, next morning, the memory of our past brought us back to the store where he bought the peaches. We went to the fruits and vegetable sections.

As soon as I saw the peaches on the shelves, I said, "No wonder they were so yummy and tasted like peaches back home." I showed the sign to Agha-jan: "organic." I said, "This section is the organic items, which are very expensive."

Agha-jan said, "No wonder I paid more for groceries yesterday." He said, "If I could read English, I would know what I am buying." Then he said, "Of course good things cost more." We never valued our fruits and vegetables back home, mostly organic; that is why we missed the sweetness of fruits and vegetables since we left Afghanistan.

Then he said, "You should teach me English."
I said, "Sure, I would love to." We were talking and walking as we left the store toward the parking lot to get the car. On the way home, he started reading the street names. I was reading them back to him the way I heard people saying it.

Then he said, "What does it mean?"

"What?"

He said this street name that we had just passed.

I said, "Dad? I do not know what it means in Dari. It is just a name."

He did not want to hear this. He said, "My daughter, it is not the right behavior. If I knew English, I wouldn't ask you!"

I felt so bad and said, "Daddy, believe me that I do not know what that street's name means."

Then he said, "Then how do you speak English with people, if you do not know the meaning of a street name?" I did not say anything. Agha-jan expected me to know everything, and he thought that my English was perfect. So, I did not know what to tell him. The quietness become oppressive, Agha-jan looking out the car window and me driving. We both were quiet. My first English teaching with Agha-jan was not successful, and the first session that he started ended with unhappiness, because I did not have an answer for his question. It was hard for me to make Agha-jan believe that my English was not as good as he thought.

We arrived home. I got a sense that Agha-jan did not want to be my student anymore.

A few days later he found an English/Dari book that was for travelers. I do not recall where and how he got that book, but I remember that he loved it.

As days passed by, I heard him complaining that he could not remember the English words that he was trying to learn. It was not only with learning the new language. I noticed sometimes he could not even remember my name.

My lovely Agha-jan. On top of all the medical issues he had, now he got to experience dementia which led to some stage of Alzheimers.

But he still loved to learn English. He was so proud of himself when he said a few words in English on the phone with people calling to advertise their services. When our phone rang, he would pick up and say, "Hello." The person would start talking and talking. Agha-jan did not understand any of what they said, and when they paused for a response, Agha-jan would say, "I no English." Some people got it that he did not know English, and they ended the conversation. But some others thought that he was saying he knew English, and they would continue talking and asking questions until Agha-jan became impatient and hung up the phone. Learning English and or any other language is not so easy, especially in older ages. When I first came to the U.S., I spoke English; but later I realized that the more you learn English, you learn that you need to learn more. English is a very sweet language, but has more than ten faces. When I say faces, I do not mean the grammar; I mean the vocabulary. One word has several meanings, especially translating documents from Dari to English or vice versa.

When I first arrived, with the level of English I knew, I thought I knew the language and that was that, unaware that my English skill was as big as a drop from a sea. English was and is my favorite language since my childhood. The beauty of this language is its levels. As soon as you learn its first level, basic speaking, basic writing and basic reading, you think that you learned English. But in fact, you need to know that is not it. This language is as huge as a sea; the farther you go in, you see that you are going deep and deeper and still have a long way to go.

In order to know how to navigate this sea, you must be created in this sea and grow in this sea to observe it in all your body. With that understanding, I decided to improve my English skills as much as I could. So, I decided to enter in this sea and add drop by drop to the drop I brought with me, until my hands got full. This process looked like a curvy path to a mountain castle, high, scary, narrow and cold to me. But during this process I had to learn not to look strange, not to sound silly and not to feel lost. On the other hand, I must watch my step, to not step on others' toes, not hurt anyone's feelings and to be clear when I communicate with people.

In order to do that and have a successful future, I had to improve my language skills. I found the nearest community college and met with a counselor who suggested I take a test to see how my English is. The next day I came back and took the test. I passed, and my score opened the door for me to start English 101. It was a great start for me. My first class was during the Ramazan, or Ramadan, month, during which Muslims practice fasting from sunrise to sunset and other forms of personal purity so as to devote themselves to prayer, charity and a heightened awareness of God. So daily, after work I had to come home, get some food, go to college and do the assignments in the car in the parking lot before going to class, and come home around nine PM and get ready for the next day.

Days, weeks and months passed. I got busier and busier with work, school, community and my life. Every day I learned a new word, something new about the new culture, something new about the new system and finally something new about the new lifestyle and how to live in a new society and new environment. As days went by, I felt comfortable with my new life and found myself in the middle of my hopes and my dreams.

Before coming to the U.S., I was escaping from persecution, from sorrow, from pain and from horror. At that time, I was in search of safety moment by moment. I was so thirsty for a calm moment to not even think about any fear, any sorrow or any type of persecutions. After coming to the U.S., I got that moment. I found that place, I saw that environment and that joy. I started living in my dream while I am awake.

With a very deep breath, I said, "Life is beautiful. I am safe."

Years passed. I lived in peace and calm and in an enjoyable environment. I worked five days a week. Work became part of my life. Workdays went so fast - meeting with clients, providing them cultural orientations, employment orientations, teaching family budgeting, navigating the health care system and the school system, finding jobs, and assisting them with their long-term goals and integration. Most of my clients' resettlement goals were so identical: they wanted to first learn English or improve their English skills and get a job, and then buy a car, buy a house, go to school and get their degree in something. It was so great to work with refugees from different countries. It was a wonderful opportunity for me to meet people of different cultures, who came from different systems, who speak different languages, who cook differently and who dress differently.

Refugees came with lots of skills and talents. Most of them came with some kind of degree and needed short term guidance from us to get integrated to this society. Some who lived all their life in the refugee camps needed a longer time of assistance in order to integrate and become self-sufficient, but their children were amazing. As soon as we enrolled them in school, they became an assistance to their parents in the path to self-sufficiency and integration. They learned English very fast and became good tutors to their families.

Living in the U.S. changed my life. As every minute passed by, life taught me that you are free, you have the right, and you can talk. Life in the U.S. did teach me that people listen to you, you are valued as a human being, you are a person.

My life looks so different from back home. My life back home died when my home was destroyed, when I lost my family members, when I was forced to leave my hometown, and when I became a refugee.

CHAPTER SEVEN

A refugee.

This name was given to me with no choice.
This name changed my life, changed my future, and stole my past.

This name carries in it several other names such as worries, fear, hopeless, stranger, poor, uncertainty and lost.

This name lived with me as soon as I crossed the Afghan - Pakistan border. I lived with this name for a few years in Pakistan.

This name introduces one as an individual who has left his or her country and is unwilling or unable to return to it because of persecution or fear of persecution (because of race, religion, membership in a particular social group, or political opinion). They leave home for safety, for asylum.

People who have experienced refugee life or homelessness or lost hope probably feel what I mean when I say I lived as a lost person. I lived in uncertainty. I was hopeless. I did not know where to go. I looked like stranger to others. My life was fearful: I was worried and frightened that any time they might make me go back to danger where I came from.

A person under refugee status is like a sick person who is seeking wellness. Sick people go to see a doctor with a heart full of hope to get treatment and get better. But if the doctor refuses to see them, what happens? Of course, they become hopeless; they do not know what to do, where to go.

Refugees lose hope when they realize that there is no place for them to live in their home and in their country. What a sad moment to know that even in your home you do not have a place to live. So, what do they need to do? They must leave. Where? They do not know. How? They do not know. But they still must leave. At that moment in time, they have two options: stay, but at the expense of your life and your loved one's life; or leave, to rescue your life and your loved one's life from danger. What you will encounter on the way to seek safety is on you. You must make this difficult decision.

Circumstances do not give too much time to plan. You need to decide fast. During these moments, the counter of your hope sets on zero. You look back, and everything looks very strange to you, everything looks cold and empty, everything tells you to go. You see that the love and the connection you had with everything around you is dead. Nothing is responding. The only think you hear is your heartbeat that tells you, "I want to be alive."

This voice makes you decide fast. There is no time. You must leave. This is the only option. You leave your home, your country, your loved ones, your school, your work, your friends, your garden, your animals, your happiness, your wealth, your memories and finally your everything, to be alive.

After coming to the end of a very scary journey and crossing international borders, with or without proper documents, you feel safe. This feeling is very temporary. Shortly after arriving in the neighboring country, you realize that it's somebody else's home, it is someone else's country, it is someone else's land. They do not want you in their home, in their country and in their land. You are an uninvited guest. They look at you as a stranger. They are afraid of you. They ask why you are there in their country. You do not know what to tell them. You feel like a bubble on the water. You feel empty inside. You look very thin from outside, like you can be destroyed with a little push. The hope for safety that you planted in your heart during your scary journey moves toward zero again.

You lost hope again. The words "lost hope" are easy to write and easy to say, but experiencing it is so difficult. It is even very hard to imagine. What would you do? They ask themselves. They do not have any answer to that question. They do not know what to do, where to go. This time they are seeking not only safety but acceptance too.

I was one of them who saw this with my eyes, felt it with my heart and touched it with my hands. When I was in Afghanistan and lived through all that fear and horror, safety was the number one priority for me.

After I arrived in Pakistan to be safe, I realized that Agha-jan and I were so alone. Alone.

This feeling was very painful; now I had to suffer differently, I thought. I needed not only safety but acceptance, too. At that time, I learned that safety and acceptance are the two most important priorities in everyone's live in order to find hope. These two go hand in hand.

I experienced losing hope another time, in different circumstances. The first time I miscarried, I lost hope, and all my dreams evaporated. My dreams. As soon I learned that I was pregnant, I was visualizing my child as a toddler in casual red sport bottoms and a blue shirt, and with a lovely smile, running and playing in our backyard which my husband built like a small garden. Yes, all those dreams left me alone. I was very disappointed and sad. At that time, I overcame that pain very quickly, because I knew that our marriage was based on acceptance. We loved each other, whether we have kids or not, whether we have money or not. We accepted that we are created for each other; wherever the journey of life takes us, we will go together. That acceptance created safety for us. I slowly, slowly came back to my normal life.

Safety and acceptance are the two big words that change people's lives. Refugees are people who do not have either. The main reason they flee and leave everything behind is that they do not feel safe. They are not wanted anywhere in the world until they get refugee status, until someone opens their door to them, until someone opens their heart to them and tells them, "Come, live with me, work with me, study with me. Come, we live on the land that God gave us. It is God's world. He created this world for us to live in, to live in peace, to live together, to love each other and accept each other."

We are all human beings, and our heart should act the same when we help people in need. But unfortunately, there are only few countries in the world that have laws to accept refugees. The United States is one of them. The Refugee Act of 1980 opened the door for refugees to resettle in the U.S. The purpose of the act was to respond to the urgent needs of persons subject to persecution in their homelands and to offer aid, asylum, and resettlement opportunities to admitted refugees. It created a standard for granting refugee status and expanded the number of refugees accepted annually in the U.S.

Agha-jan and I resettled to the U.S. as refugees under the refugee act of 1980. We felt safe and accepted in the U.S. We entered this country as the law permitted us.

When we lived in Afghanistan and Pakistan under a very difficult time, I always hoped that a miracle would happen and rescue us from that situation. During those times, I always thought about my relatives who escaped Afghanistan during the communist regime or the early Mujahedeen regime and got themselves to safe places like Europe and the U.S. But I never knew that while yet, they lived in safety, they lost what they will never get again: the unity of family, the love, the trust, and the happiness. The war in the Afghan nation not only destroyed homes, schools, factories, hospitals and the entire country. It destroyed the people's lives. Families got separated, not by their choice. One went to Iran, another went to Pakistan, the other one went to Russia.

Some went to Europe or the U.S. Are they going to see each other again? Probably not. Will history remember the war? Probably yes. But will anyone remember and tell the story of the people's plight? Probably not. Will someone, honestly? Maybe, if the refugees themselves are willing to relive their pain, fear and heartbreak to share their stories.

Separation from loved ones is something that people do not think about when their life is in danger and they must make a vital decision. That night Agha-jan and I decide to leave our home in search for safety, we had a few minutes to decide to leave. At that moment, all we were thinking was our life. We did not think about who we would leave behind and what we would lose by making that quick decision. Refugees are people who do not feel safe in their own homes. They first leave their home and want to find a safe place in their city. If they cannot find a safe place in their city, they find their way to another town or city where they hope to be safe and return home soon; but in a lot of situations, those people had to even leave their entire country because they could not quickly find even a hand-sized space and environment in their country to shelter and breathe safely there. They leave their home, and, as a last resort, leaving their country is the only option for them, just to be alive.

After they reach safety and look back, then they realize what they lost. Of course, all values, all happiness, all hopes, all respect and all love that they used to have with their people, they may never get again from strangers. I experienced that feeling personally, the day we arrived in Pakistan. I felt that I was in a bubble. There was no war, no persecution against women; but nothing was mine. I was a very stranger to their streets, to their city, to their people and to their culture. I was an unwanted person there. I had no value, no happiness, no hope, no respect and no love there. I felt safe at that moment, but I knew that I am no one anymore.

But it was not long before I realized that not only was I no one anymore, but that security or safety was not real, either, for us in Pakistan.

Of course, when we came to the U.S., it was not like that for me. Upon arrival, I felt that I would find my way someday to be someone here. The U.S. is the land of opportunities. That night when our plane was getting closer and closer to landing, the beautiful lights of Arizona and Phoenix city were calling to me: "Come, here is your home; you will not feel a stranger anymore." I immediately thought I was alive again. But even though I believed that I had come to a safe country, it was still very hard to believe how I would live here. It was the reality, and I even felt safe and accepted by the law to enter the U.S. and live here, but I still worried that if people did not want me and look at me as a stranger, what should I do? I told myself, "You need time. You need to know people, and let people around you get to know you."

Several years after living in the U.S., I remembered this thought, "You need time. You need to know people, and let people around you get to know you." This memory came back to me and helped a lot when I had a smart coworker who knew her job very well, and I was very new to that organization and was working so hard to perform my job to the best of my ability. That coworker was like a shadow on my desk, watching how I did my work, what time I went to break, how I responded to customers, what mistakes I made, and so on. But at the same time, I got my first recognition from management for the good work I was doing. I decided to keep doing my work and ignore her behavior. One day I learned that I had to go on a business trip with a couple others, including that person. After work, we went to see the city. We got lost for a few seconds, and after finding our way, we laughed a lot. In a few days, we came back to work. She said, "I want to talk with you."

I said to myself, "Oh, what did I do this time? Maybe I went to get some coffee this morning, and I forget to tell them where I was going?"
As soon as I sat with her at the table, she said, "I am really happy to work with you, and I am so sorry that I did not know you before. You are a very good person."
I was so surprised, and I wondered what I did that now I am a good person! I said, "Thank you; I am glad to be part of this team."

From that day until she left that job, she was so good to me. I gave time to myself and to her, for her to get to know me. I never complained about her, even though sometimes I felt it was too much for me. I kept explaining to myself that I was new to this job. It is normal that people would react to my work style and have to listen closely to my English as a second language. Maybe it was not my work style but my English and my strong accent that bothered some people. With all those explanations to myself, I was able to give time to myself to let things go.

Of course, people who have never traveled outside the U.S. and have never been around foreigners need some time to learn about who we are, why we came here. Some people do not know the U.S. immigration laws; so if they react, I should not be surprised.

The U.S. refugee resettlement programs around the country have an important role, not only providing services to refugees but also to educate the community. Who is a refugee? Why do they come to the U.S.? That information raises public awareness that refugees are coming to the U.S. legally, and that they have the right to work, to study, and to be part of this society.

This information is an indirect request that if you see refugees in your community, it is your role as a neighbor, as a colleague, as a class mate, as a friend, and finally, as a countryman to assist them on their path to self-sufficiency and to integration into the new system and new society.

The majority of Americans do not know about the Refugee Act of 1980, the current refugee admission policy, the refugee program services and the programs in their states. They don't understand who refugees are and why refugees come to their country. These questions will be answered if you talk with a refugee who is your neighbor, your coworker, your class mate. When you see a refugee in a park and their children come toward your kids to play together, just ask them where they come from, what language they speak. If they speak English, good; you will hear a beautiful accent. If they do not speak English and do not understand you, you will see a pleasant attitude and a smiley face that says "Sorry, no English."

Agha-jan used this term a lot. He loved to communicate with people, but his English ability made it very hard for him to talk with people. Sometimes he wished Americans would speak his language. We would laugh, and I would tell him, "Come on, Dad."

Agha-jan and I continued to enjoy our freedom and our new life in the U.S. The first few years were amazing. Agha-jan was able to quit smoking. This was a big accomplishment for him. We bought a single-family house. It was our first home in the U.S. I became so busy with remodeling the house with new flooring and new paint, buying new furniture, new area rugs and decorating the house with Afghan-style curtains and some table decorations.

Agha-jan kept very busy with gardening and making our front and back yard like a garden. One day I came from work and saw beautiful flowers were planted in our front yard. I wondered about it and asked myself, "Who did this? My father? No, he cannot. He is sick and should not even try to do this." I rushed from the driveway to the house. I saw he had company, a man from Afghanistan. After greeting them, I said to my Agha-jan, "Flowers?"

He asked me, "Do you like them?"

"Yes, but how did you plant them? You should not bend your back."

He smiled and turned to his friend and said, "Look at my worrier daughter."

Then he looked at me and said, "My daughter, I wish I could carry things. Your uncle," - he referred to his friend who was sitting on our new couch – "he planted them."

I said, "Oh, thank you so much."

He said, "It is ok. Tomorrow, I will do the back yard for him; it is a fun project."

In a few days our yard looked so beautiful. Every day after coming home from work, Agha-jan and I enjoyed the beauty of our backyard by watering and watching the green lawn, the roses and all the other beautiful flowers. Sometimes, Agha-jan asked me to bring him his green tea and sugar cane while he was sitting outside.

Our life was so beautiful, but among all those beauties, we were so much alone. No one from our family, no relatives, not even any distant relatives were near. We were an example of a bird in golden cage.

We were very connected with the Afghan community. We both found great friends. But still, no one from our family was around. I miss those moments that I spent with my aunt and uncles from my mother's side and my Agha-jan's side. I miss the time that I spent with my lovely cousins, a little younger, my age, a little older, some older, and some a lot older. I loved them all. They were my role models. I had a few cousins who were engineers; others were medical doctors. A few others were teachers, a couple of them were pilots, and a bunch of them were in schools and universities. Education was very important in my family and among my relatives.

The Afghan society's gender principle, while consistent in letter, varies greatly in the way different regions and families apply it. Under some governments, women had very few rights, even contradicting Islam itself. Under other constitutions or rulers, women were allowed freedom of dress and education as well as other societal freedoms. My family had its own rules, like most urban Afghans. Both girls and boys must go to school and complete their educations. Both boys and girls must participate in housework. Both girls and boys had the right to choose their future spouses, but with their family's agreement.

My cousins were my Agha-jan's friends; or I can say, Agha-jan was one of their favorite uncles. So, I knew that Agha-jan missed all his nephews and nieces as well as his siblings.

One of his childhood stories he thought was funny. He said that it was Ramazan month in Kabul, and he was 10 years old. His aunt gave him ten Afghani and asked him to fast one day instead of her. So he did. And during the day, while he was fasting, he went out and used that ten Afghani and bought chickpeas. The shopkeeper filled his two pockets with salted chickpeas. On the way home, while he was eating and enjoying those delicious chickpeas, his older brother saw him. The older brother immediately asked him, "Why are you not fasting for our aunt?"

Agha-jan said, "As soon as I heard that, I started crying and begging him to not tell my aunt." Now he made a deal with his older brother to keep this secret. On their return, his brother asked him to do the hand washing tasks for dinner which was his daily tasks before and after lunch and dinner. In Afghanistan, it is very important to wash one's hands before and after eating food. During that time in Afghanistan, not every house had a sink. Instead, every family had a mobile sink - basically, a couple dishes. In one, they carried water; that one looked like a big teapot. The other is the big bowl that the hand washing water goes into. The youngest child of the family was responsible make that ready and bring it to everyone to wash their hands before eating food. It is very hard work for even a ten year old. My poor Agha-jan!

After hearing that story, I wondered why he had to fast for an adult person when he was only 10 years old. I still do not agree that an adult should ask a child to fast a whole day for her. But still, for my Agha-jan, it was a memory, and he lived with all his memories and his past. But gradually, sometimes when he was telling me stories from his childhood, he paused for a second and said, "I do not remember what happened then."

The war in Afghanistan took away all the beauty of life from us. I lost my beautiful mother, who taught me to love everyone and never think you are better than others, no matter even if you are the wealthiest person in the world, no matter even if you are the president of the world, no matter even if you are the prettiest girl in the world. She taught me to follow the good and stay away from the bad.

My mother was a very pretty woman. She was a good cook, too. She made noodles from scratch, then she cooked them with ground meet and beans, and then she decorated the dish with fresh yogurt, olive oil and some ground dried mint. It was delicious. I have not had that delicious dish for more than two decades now. No one can cook that food the way she cooked. She also made orange palo (zerda palo). Not every woman knows how to make zerda palo the right way. Zerda palo is a yummy Afghan main dish that contains rice and is served with meat, the skin of sour orange, and some almonds and pistachios. She cooked that dish when there was a special occasion in our house.

My sister was a good cook, too, but she was very busy with her school and painting. My sister was a very good artist. She made beautiful paintings. She never went to any course or training; it was a talent that God gave her. One day when she was in seventh grade, she got an award from our province governor. While he visited her school, he went to the class where my sister was studying. The governor got the white chalk and drew one side of a vase on the blackboard and asked, "Who can draw the other side of this vase to make it complete?" Of course, drawing a vase, for my sister, was a piece of cake. She raised her hand, went to the blackboard on the wall, and got the white chalk. With lots of confidence, she started drawing the other side of the vase. In a couple minutes, she drew the entire vase with its shadow on a surface. The governor said, "Excellent. This was more than I expected. Good job."

But the war took her from me. I lost my beautiful sister and my hero brother. He was just a handsome young man. He was a very good friend of my sister. They studied together, they painted together, and sometimes they sang a song together. He was so friendly; almost every neighbor loved him. He helped our neighbors clean their roofs of snow during the winter. If he saw a neighbor woman or an elderly person carrying heavy things, he ran to help them. He was a hero not only in our family, but to our neighbors.

The Afghan war took them from us. Agha-jan and I did not want to talk with each other about them. We talked with ourselves and reviewed our memories in solitude. We cried separately. That war took our lives, our loved ones, our home, our happiness, our hope, our future, and our everything. We did not want to talk with each other about our past, because we did not want to remind each other of who we were and who we had. We both wanted to hide our past from each other and live in the present.

Our backyard flowers were blooming, and those flowers with their pleasing colors and smells became the medicine of our soul.

Look what our own country did to us in Afghanistan. They took millions of Afghans' lives. They forced millions of Afghans to leave the country. They took people's happiness. They took our citizenship rights, and finally they destroyed our country.

But, here on this side of the globe, people sit at a table and write a refugee act, and every year allocate funds to support refugees, assist refugees, teach them their language and their system, and help them integrate in their society. The U.S. Refugee Resettlement Act of 1980 saved our lives and opened its country's doors and sheltered us, giving us all the rights that each U.S. citizen has.

That decision, that was made and turned into an act, saved my life and my Agha-jan's life and has allowed millions of other people like us to be safe.

Now, we must find a way to escape from being alone. How? Where to go? Who can help? You are safe but alone. You are safe, but you have lost half of your life which you cannot get again. The only way I could escape from that loneliness was to become me.

During all these year in the U.S. I met wonderful people. I made lots of friends. Most of them are from Afghanistan and had just arrived as refugees and lived nearby when we first came to the U.S.

This friendship helps our mind to not feel isolated. We share the same culture and language. At least that can help to relieve me from feeling isolated. So, I started meeting with a few of them. They, like me, know the pain that every person went through during the war in Afghanistan.

Even though we came from the same country and share a lot of similarities, there are some background differences among us. For example, I have a few friends that came from wealthy families and some others from not so wealthy. They have different education levels; for example, some have higher education, some are high school graduates, and others have a 10th or 11th grade education. Higher education was a number one dream for every Afghan girl and woman in Afghanistan. The first obstacle for a lot of women that were not able to complete their high school or college was the long war in Afghanistan. The second obstacle was the Afghan traditional society that me, my friends and millions of other Afghan girls lived in. In some families, the father and brothers did not like or want their daughters or sisters to continue their education beyond elementary. Those traditional men believed that girls are created to live in the house, do the housework, get married, become a mother and raise children.

Thus, our friendships began based on being compatriots, not based on being on the same education level or having the same family background. It is so many years now that we have been friends. We respect each other, and we support each other during good and bad days.

Sometimes I think about my friends back home. I did not have as many friends there as I have in the U.S. They were few, but I always remember them. The last time I saw my best friend from high school was the day we went to get our final government entrance exam for college. That day I found out that my school matched the engineer's college and hers the economic college. We were friends since 4th grade. I did not see her after that day. In college, I made two other friends. One became my best friend, and the other became a good friend as well.

The last day I saw them was in our university. That day, we spoke about the rumor we heard that a new government was coming, and one of its policies was that it would not let women study and work outside of the home. One of my friends said, "This is a rumor; let's not think about this." We were walking on the beautiful grounds of our university. It was an autumn day; the ground was covered by the dry leaves from the old trees. While we were walking on those leaves, they sounded like chewing crispy potato chips. We were walking, but in the back of our heads we were carrying some unknown worries. We did not look like before. That day, like every day we took the bus from the bus station across from our university street to go home. In the bus, the driver played a song from Ahmad Zahir who was singing, "I am determined to travel with a sweet grief." The appeal of Ahmad Zahir's music crossed age and societal boundaries, making him Afghanistan's one and only superstar, the "Elvis of Afghanistan"! His sad story and the suspicious circumstances of his death added to his appeal. His car crashed on his 33rd birthday, after he was apparently lured out of the city. His political views did not align with the Marxist government of the time, and he had had an affair with the daughter of a powerful man. Either had reason to want him gone, but no one knows what really happened. All we knew was that he was gone too soon, on his birthday, and on the day his baby daughter was born. He left a young son as well, adding to the sadness and the appeal.

Though we did not realize it, the words he sang in the bus that day would be prophetic for us, a few young girls with their whole bright future ahead of them. The bus arrived at Kabul's downtown center. We left the bus and said goodbye to each other, and each took different buses to go home. That goodbye was our last word we said to each other. After that day I never saw them again, and I never heard from them.

That rumor that we were talking about on the way home became a bitter truth. The next day the entire country got a new face. A new regime came into power and changed our lives. I do not know what happened to my lovely friends. I do not know if they are even alive. I missed Frozan's laughing, and I missed Wahida's sense of humor. We knew each other's funny language. We named our classmates, without letting them know; we were talking about them in front of them with the names we gave them. They did not know who we are talking about. We went to the college library together. We escaped from Algebra classes most of the time, because we did not like our professor. He was so serious; if you came one minute late, he would not let you in the class.

Our friendship back home was so simple and straightforward. We were the same age, had the same education level, and most of the time were from the same city.

The war took all those beauties, all those trusts, all that love and all that honesty from us. The long war damaged the Afghan roots which will need a hundred years to revive. We lost each other. My last word to those lovely girls was a goodbye during that autumn day. That day we never thought we would disappear from each other for ever.

It was not a dream. It was real. We disappeared from each other the next day. I heard that during the beginning of the communist regime a lot of people disappeared and never came back home. Their family did not know what happened to them. People left home in the morning to go to work or college but never came back. Lots of people were kidnapped from their home and never came back. So, during different times, people experienced separation differently. One lost his son, another lost her father, others lost their brother, uncle, aunt, sister, mother, daughter, friends, coworkers, neighbor. Millions of Afghans lost each other in the past few decades. Millions of Afghans were killed during the Russian war, during the Mujahedeen war, during the Taliban war. Hundreds of Afghans were kidnaped during the communist regimes, during the Mujahedeen regimes, during the Taliban regimes. Millions of Afghans were displaced internally and lost their homes. Millions of Afghans became refugees to Iran, Pakistan, Tajikistan, Uzbekistan, India, Germany, Turkey, Holland, Finland, Sweden, Denmark, Canada, Australia, Austria, the United Kingdom, the U.S. and many more countries. Millions of Afghans became addicted to drugs and became useless people for themselves and for their families. Millions of Afghans lost their leg, hands or other parts of their bodies, and millions of Afghans lost their education opportunity.

Agha-jan and I are some of those people who tasted the bitterness and the pain of war. We lost family members. Agha-jan was injured in his back; he lost his job. I lost my school. And we were finally driven from our homeland by our countrymen for being Afghan citizens.

Living in the U.S. has changed my life. Every passing minute of life reminds me that I am free, I have rights, and I can talk. Life in the U.S. has taught me that people listen to you; you are valued as a human being; you are a person.

My life here looks so different from my life back home. My life back home passed away the day that my home was destroyed, the day that I lost my family members, and the day that I was forced to leave my hometown and become a refugee. A refugee. My second name. This name lives with me, comes to work with me, and goes home with me. This name and this status are tied to my life.

CHAPTER EIGHT

This was a summary of my history. I know there are lots of people in the world that went through worse than I did.

So why did I write my story today?

To increase more donations for refugees? No.

To feel bad for those people and give them temporary shelter? No.

So why did I write my history? Why do I want people to read it at least one time?

I wrote the history of my life to let people know how the war in Afghanistan changed my life.

On the first days of my arrival in the U.S., I compared the currency's value when I was shopping; for example, buying a bag of potatoes here would buy a couple kilograms of meat in Afghanistan. It started from there. That comparing mode continued to remind me who I was and who I am.

When I left Afghanistan, I lost everything. I left my home and the cold breeze touching my face. I lost my memories and my hope. I became a refugee, persecuted, unable and unwilling to return. This is true. The war destroyed my country, my city and my home, and separated families.

Now I have everything… but not that morning breeze, not that comfort, not those food flavors, not the family. I became like a bird who has wings but cannot fly to see the nest that I was born in. Maybe the nest is not there anymore; maybe the tree was burned; maybe the city has a different look. The people there might look at me as a stranger.

One day when I came home from work, Agha-jan looked so happy and told me, "Look we can see Kabul, our city, in TV!" He was changing the channels and then realized that it was on YouTube. There was a short video of Kabul city with an Afghan song in the background. We sat and watched that song. Our beautiful Kabul. He spent his days watching those videos.

I knew that he missed Kabul a lot, but he did not want to go back. First, his health was not good; second, he knew that Kabul is not his childhood Kabul anymore.

One day, when I entered to his room to wake him up to give him his medication, I found him unresponsive. That day, Agha-jan left me alone in this big world. My Agha-jan, my hero, died. This was another big loss in my life.

In Afghanistan, people had family-owned cemetery land. The long war in Afghanistan took that right and denied the wishes of its citizens to buried next to each other after they died.

Agha-jan is buried in southwest of the U.S. His older sister was buried in the northwest of the U.S. One of his brothers is buried in the northeast of the U.S. His other brother is buried in Canada, another brother is buried in Pakistan, and his youngest sister is buried in Pakistan, while their parents are buried in Afghanistan.

So, Afghanistan's long war has not only forced us to flee but made us to flee forever.

How beautiful is to be born, grow up, get old and die in your country of origin, where people never call you by a status, such as asylee, refugee, or immigrant.

How beautiful is to go to an elementary school, a high school and a college that people around you know, schools whose names do not sound unfamiliar to the people in your life.

How beautiful is to work in a place where everyone speaks your language. And whenever you speak, people do not look at you strangely because you speak with an accent.

How beautiful it is if, at your workplace, you understand people, especially when they use an idiom during their talking. The first time I heard "an elephant in the room," I wondered what it meant. I could not make the connection. An elephant in the room?

How beautiful it is to live in an area where you know all your neighbors; you trust each other; your kids play together; you drink tea with their parents; and you are there for each other on the good days and bad days.

A refugee who had to scape Afghanistan in search of safety will never find these beauties in their life again unless they fall under one of the three options of the durable solution and return home. I lost some of these beauties as soon as I crossed the international border and arrived in Pakistan.

AFTERWORD

Dear world leaders, the world legislators, and the governments:

Your people are the asset of your country. They hold your culture, the legacy of your past. They hold your beautiful language; they hold your ancient history, and they hold the proficiency and skills that others do not have.

Do not let anyone persecute, harm or torture your asset.

Do not let anyone uproot them and make them leave their homes.

Do not let anyone force your asset to leave you and become someone else's asset.

Afghan famous Poet Jalal al-Din Rumi was once a twelve-year-old refugee when his family emigrated from Balkh – Afghanistan. They had to escape the Genghis Khan's imminent threat and started on their westward odyssey. He is buried in Turkey.

This is one big example of assets that is now the pride of a country not their homeland, assets lost to the land of their birth.

Dear world leaders, legislatures and governments: Please let your people, the asset of your country, travel to other countries to explore the differences of other places. In Afghanistan we say, "The drum sounds are nice from a distance." Some people dream to explore the first world countries to study, to visit, or even to work. Give them the opportunity.

Dear world leaders, legislatures and governments: When refugees arrive on your soil, help them to restart their life again. Do not close your door on them. They seek refuge in you. Listen to them. Each one has a story to tell. No one want to leave their home, their loved ones, unless they must.

Dear world leaders, legislatures and governments: You can turn this planet into a safe home where no one will have to leave their home and seek refuge in a neighbors' house.

Absolutely, you can make big differences in the world so that no one, like me and my late Agha-jan, has to count the minutes and wait for the darkness of the night to change its color to daylight until we find the moment to leave our home, to escape from our city and our country, to seek safety.

Dear world leaders, legislatures and governments: For sure, you can plant the tree of peace in the world so that no like me feels that they live in a cage and wishes for wings to fly to the sky in search of safety.

Dear world leaders, legislatures and governments:
I will end my book with this sentence.

Do not make a person be humiliated to get the peace that God has given him.

ACKNOWLEDGEMENTS

To my Agha-jan (Noor M. Hamkar), I miss you more than words can say. Thank you for making this hard journey with me. I wish you could be here with me to see this dream become a reality.

To my husband and family, your support through this project and the love you have shown me has been amazing. Thank you for being there for me and believing in my dreams.

To all the friends and family who have supported me in this journey and been a part of this amazing story, thank you! My story would be incomplete without you in it.

Tereasa Shepherd, thank you for taking my story and making it so wonderful. Your contribution to this project as my editor was invaluable.

Britney Thompson, thank you for all the work you put into the design of my book to make it beautiful and professional. You truly made the publishing process simple and enjoyable.

To the U.S. government, thank you for the Refugee Act & Resettlement program. The work you are doing in this world is making a difference.

ABOUT THE AUTHOR

Asmeen Hamkar was born in Afghanistan, where she studied civil engineering in Kabul Polytechnic University until forced to flee her war-torn homeland. This book is the story of her escape. It talks about the journey she went through in search of safety. Her message to the world governments, leaders, and legislatures is that they can turn this planet into a safe place where no one will have to leave their home and seek refuge in a neighbor's house.

She currently lives in the U.S. where she assists refugees in their path to self-sufficiency and successful resettlement. This is her first book and she looks forward to writing further books about Afghanistan and her life there.